# One Shovel Full

## Telling Stories to Change Beliefs, Attitudes, & Perceptions

*by*
**Brad Fregger**

**F&F Publishing**
Austin, Texas

# One Shovel Full

By Brad Fregger
© Brad Fregger, 2003
F&F Publishing
A Division of 1st World Library
8015 Shoal Creek Blvd., Suite 100
Austin, TX 78737
512-339-4000
www.1stworldlibrary.com

*2nd Printing*

Senior Editor
Barbara Foley

Editorial Assistance
Jon Fregger
Barry Silverberg
David Schlosser

Cover Design & Production
Mark Miyaji

Author Services
1st World Library

Printing & Binding
Books On Demand

Library of Congress Catalog Number: 2003092273
ISBN: 0-9718562-1-4

All rights reserved. No part of this book may be reproduced or utilized in any form or by any means, electronic, or mechanical, including photocopying, or recording, or by an information storage and retrieval system, without permission in writing from the author.

**Books by Brad Fregger**

*Published by Sunstar Publishing*

**Lucky That Way**
Stories of Seizing the Moment While Creating the Games Millions Play

*Published by F&F Publishing*

**Get Things Done**
Ten Secrets of Creating and Leading Exceptional Teams

**One Shovel Full**
Telling Stories to Change Beliefs, Attitudes, & Perceptions

*To*
**Barbara,**
my wife and partner,
in anticipation and celebration
of stories yet to come

# Preface

Stories have their greatest impact on the subconscious. They change people in subtle, indirect ways that have a surprisingly profound effect on them, both as individuals and as members of a group.

Perhaps this is why my most popular workshop is *One Shovel Full – Telling Stories to Effect Change in Individuals and Organizations*. Year after year, this topic is the favorite over other workshops and seminars I offer on a broad variety of subjects, including: *Storytelling, Handling Traumatic Change, The Internet's Technical Challenge, Effective Leadership, Hiring Exceptional People, Getting Things Done*, and *Creativity*.

I believe that my storytelling workshop's success comes from the fact that my background and education is extremely varied. This allows me to view things from many different perspectives. Within these pages, I will share through the prism of personal experience rather than from knowledge garnered as the result of academic research, interviews with storytelling experts, or any other outside source.

This book's focus is how stories work on the subconscious and how they can lead to life changes. While this has been known for thousands of years, most people do not apply this knowledge - especially educators, speakers, and ministers.

This is not a history of storytelling nor a guide on how to tell a story to "capture" an audience. Instead, it is my hope that you will be enlightened by information about storytelling that is not readily available elsewhere.

I want to share my stories so that you will share yours. Every story in this book resulted in a learning for me, even those that seem to be purely entertaining. The best way to share that learning is by telling the story.

Stories are our links with our past, our present and our posterity. Take full ownership of this book. Make it work for you by making it yours. Then I hope you will begin creating the stories that tell your unique life learnings, thus helping make this a better world for those whose lives you touch.

Jot down your thoughts and share them with me. Also share your stories with me. Perhaps we can find a way to share them with more readers in the future.

You can send your stories to:

Brad Fregger
brad@1stworldlibrary.com

My hope is that you will enjoy reading these stories as much as I have enjoyed sharing them.

Brad Fregger
Austin, Texas
April 2002.

# Contents

## ONE SHOVEL FULL

Page #

| | |
|---|---|
| Preface | 1 |
| Contents | 3 |
| Foreword | 5 |
| Thanks | 9 |
| Introduction | 11 |

### PART ONE – THE POWER OF STORIES

| | |
|---|---|
| 1. How the Mind Works | 17 |
|    - *Where's David?* | 19 |
|    - *Where'd She Come From?* | 21 |
|    - *It Works Like Human Intuition* | 24 |
| 2. How Stories Work | 27 |
|    - *Parable Proof* | 30 |
|    - *Nobody Was Interested* | 34 |

### PART TWO – ENTERTAINING STORIES

| | |
|---|---|
| 3. Tall Tale of Turtles | 39 |
| 4. Danny's Story | 41 |
| 5. Almost a Messiah | 45 |
| 6. This is Our Teacher | 51 |
| 7. Hall of Fame | 57 |
| 8. Chihoe's Story | 61 |
| 9. Short Stories | 65 |
|    - *Customer Service Plus* | 65 |
|    - *Where's My Suit?* | 66 |
|    - *Percentage Error* | 67 |
|    - *Daddy's Very Busy* | 68 |
|    - *Is That Seat Taken?* | 69 |

PART THREE – INSPIRATIONAL STORIES

| | |
|---|---|
| 10. One Shovel Full | 73 |
| 11. Shanghai | 79 |
| 12. My Heroes | 89 |
| 13. The Garden of Eden | 97 |
| 14. Grandma's Poem | 101 |

PART FOUR – LIFE STORIES

| | |
|---|---|
| 15. My Life | 107 |
| 16. Fregger's Law | 115 |
| 17. Solitaire | 121 |
| 18. Oh, Shit! | 125 |
| 19. This Isn't Funny | 131 |
| 20. Stranger Than Fiction | 141 |

PART FIVE – LIFE-CHANGING STORIES

| | |
|---|---|
| 21. Creating the Story | 149 |
| - *It Was a Hoot!* | 153 |
| 22. Good News | 155 |
| 23. The Story of Fred | 159 |
| 24. The Miracle Man | 165 |
| 25. Auntie Perry | 171 |

| | |
|---|---|
| Contact | 175 |
| Author's Bio | 177 |

# *Foreword*

*I* fell in love with Anne Robinson the first time we met. She is a curious person indeed; and upon discovering my web site, she wrote me an email suggesting we meet. Shortly thereafter, I found myself at her home discussing all manner of things; or as Anne put it, "we had a mutual broadcasting network." The next day I realized I wanted Anne to write my Foreword. Her knowledge of creativity and inspiration made her the perfect candidate ... the only problem ... I had already asked Michael McGar, the President of Alchemy Studios (and one of the most creative people I have ever known) and he had already agreed.

Still I felt compelled to ask Anne. So I called her, and she said yes, too.

My wife Barbie said, "What are you going to do now?"

"Who made the rule that a book could only have one Foreword?" I responded. "This book will have two."

Anne's Foreword arrived two days later and I loved it. Then Michael called and said his Foreword was ready.

As I read Michael's words, it dawned on me that his piece wasn't a Foreword at all; it was an Introduction. The Introduction I had written was the weakest link in the book by far; I was almost embarrassed to include it. But here was an Introduction I could be proud of. This is another lesson of trusting my guidance and then having it all fall beautifully into place. Here's Anne's Foreword:

Brad Fregger, the man, offers a broad field for exploration. His personal charm is deepened by wide knowledge and spiritual conviction. And these personal facets gain added brilliance in the stories he collects, remembers, or originates.

However, the stories, not the man telling them, are the focus of this intriguing volume. *One Shovel Full* is an unusual collection of anecdotes from Fregger's life, stories he has told to meet the needs of a large variety of life situations: from entertaining an audience, to retaining a restless employee, to saving a troubled relationship. The title comes from a memorable experience with his son Jeff, which gave Dad/Brad a great story of inspiration, not to mention a big lesson.

Fregger has gathered these episodes like pearls from the oysters of his own life discoveries. Currently he teaches MBA students at Saint Edward's University in Austin, Texas. He has seriously studied hypnotism; has been operations manager of a Mervyn's Store in Mountain View, California; a Chief Product Officer for Austin's Dryken Technologies; a Director of Training and Development for the Atari Corporation (at which time he studied Neuro Linguistic Programming, NLP). He was intrigued with the training methods of Robert Blake and Jane Mouton, Austin's famous Scientific Methods duo. And the list goes on ... and on.

In fact, each story-pearl in the book has been extracted with Fregger's sharp knife of relevance from a different oyster-event. The anecdotes he shares are many and varied. He offers them to his readers for their own reading and heeding or as models for creating their own pearls of wisdom.

Brad has divided his storybook into several parts. He first talks with the reader about the Power of Stories. Part Two deals with Entertaining Stories; Part Three with Inspirational Stories; Part Four with Life Stories; and Part Five with Life-Changing Stories.

I highly recommend that you approach this literary fare as a very rich, tasty food. After the first forkful you'll be tempted into one long, quick gobble. That can lead only to literary indigestion. So turn this marvel-meal into a several-course repast. Eat slowly. Savor flavors. And between each major division, cleanse your palate.

Then let the many fine recountings in *One Shovel Full* awaken you to the beauty and bounty of your own story material; not just tales about you, your family, your friends, but the myriad stories from all aspects of your world.

Learn, as Brad has, to tell those anecdotes with full understanding of their meaning and worth. But don't explain or ask your listeners/readers their reactions. Let the unfettered subconscious mind have time to work its own magic.

I have on the wall in front of me a big make-believe snowflake from last year's Christmas card. It is gorgeously iridescent. Every altered light beam brings out a different color play. Stories refract subconscious light the same way. Each individual subconscious then supplies its own radiant sum-of-all-the-parts for the conscious mind to enjoy.

---

*Anne Robinson's Profile:*

**Anne Durrum Robinson** *is an 88 year-old Texan who has taught creativity for 20 years. Prior to her work as an consultant, she spent 10 years with the State of Texas.*

*Her clients include business, industry, government and academia. Her speaking engagements and travels have taken her through all 50 states and 35 countries.*

*She has received regional, national and international awards for poetry, plays, song lyrics and light-verse books. Recent honors include:*

**Liz Carpenter Lifetime Achievement Award** *from Austin Chapter of the Association for Women in Communications*

**National Headliner Award** *(one of two) from the National Association for Women in Communications*

**Lifetime Achievement Award** *for Innovation from Innovation Network (one of four)*

**Special Certificate** *from Intuition Network (first ever given) for work in teaching intuition to business*

# *Thanks*

*I* have many people to thank for being a part of the *One Shovel Full* story. Those I'm aware of at this moment are:

First, Anne Robinson for her wonderful Foreword and Michael McGar for an Introduction, far better than one I attempted.

Of course, the "team" who helped produce it:

> Senior Editor: Barbara Foley
> Editorial Assistance: Jon Fregger, Barry Silverberg, and David Schlosser
> Cover Design & Production: Mark Miyaji

And then there are those who shared stories with me:

> Jon Fregger           Chihoe Hahn
> Jeff Fregger          Mary-Ann Fregger
> Dennis Fregger        Barbara Foley
> Bryn Chernek

Then, those who read it early and told me what worked and what didn't.

> Stephen Balkum        Claudia Bilan
> Lori Balkum           Nancy Grady
> Paula Sandige         Margaret Baacke

And finally, my daughter Bryn who happily served as a sounding board for my stories as I struggled to get them to sound, and read, just right.

# Introduction

Since the beginning of time, stories have taught and inspired us. The first cave paintings, hands and lyrical animals blown and scratched on walls, were the first written stories; people recording their experiences and instructing future generations of what they had learned. People are drawn to stories and storytellers. We first learn about our world as babies through nursery rhymes and fables that shape our understanding of good and bad, sweet and bitter. Grimm's collection of stories was a chronicle of some of the scariest stories about children of the time; yet they are still the standard today, though edited to excerpt some of the most heinous anti-Semitism.

What Brad has done in these pages is to point out and make clear the true power of the story. He shows how stories well told can alter our firmly held beliefs, make us buy things we hadn't considered, vote for someone we don't know. Film directors are today's most visible storytellers and get paid millions to tell us really good stories. However, there are other storytellers among us who create compelling images and exert strong influence over our lives: game designers, commercial producers, songwriters, sitcom writers, and political image-makers, to name a few. All exert a huge influence over us, and we revel in the experience.

Few people understand the subtle power of a story. Thus they rob it of its power by following the typical educational and speech model: Tell them what you're going to tell them, tell them, then tell them what you've told them. Brad's rule is "NOT to explain why you are telling the story and what you hope the person will gain from it. Additionally, it's very important NOT to ask questions like, "What have you learned from this story?'" Recently a grad student of Brad's who is a teacher asked, "What are you talking about? I'd loose my job or be criticized by the administration if I don't follow those standards."

The current standards for "teaching excellence" require educators to ask those kinds of questions. But that doesn't change the fact that speaking to the conscious mind jeopardizes the learning opportunity. Sadly, the ignorance about how we learn through storytelling is pervasive in education and industry. As a teacher and chairman of a college department, I learned that education is show business, as are most other pursuits involving contact with other humans. In order to be successful as a teacher or salesman or CEO, you must hold the attention of the audience and involve them in your story. The fact is, most people have yet to understand that simple truth.

Effective storytelling, as Brad illustrates in this book, is the core of communication and persuasion. Telling what the story is about, then telling the story, then explaining it afterward is a sure path to the destruction of effective persuasion. Have you ever heard a great standup comic tell you what the joke is going to be about, then tell the joke and then explain what it means? NO! The sure sign of a badly told joke is the explanation at then end, "I guess you had to be there." Songs, poetry, novels, and movies, as well as other forms of "storytelling," don't explain the message. But I never realized why it was so important not to do so. Brad sheds light on this little understood subject.

Brad has been at the center of several storytelling ventures and will, over time, be in the center of more, simply because he can tell a story. I also tell many stories and was not conscious of how I used stories to create influence until I read Brad's book; the unconscious application of a conscious tool. Brad and I both have to ask our associates repeatedly, "Have you heard this story before?" Stories are so much a part of how we lead and instruct that several stories are available for each situation. How do you deal with a bad employee? How do you deal with a thief for a partner? How do people deal with loss? When is it right to brag? What does blind faith do? How desperate do people get in bad times? What is courage? What is determination? All these questions have answers in parables, Aesop's Fables, Bre'r Rabbit, Brad's Turtles.

Building on this foundation, Brad explores the art of storytelling. Stories of all kinds follow. Most stories are from his own experience, or created for various purposes. The stories you read here are designed to entertain, teach, inspire, and change people's beliefs, attitudes, and perceptions in positive ways, ways that increase their potential. Reading Brad's collection of stories has inspired me to write down some of my stories, and I hope reading his stories will inspire you, too, to begin writing down your own stories.

Did I ever tell you the one about the redneck and his midget brother in a bar fight at the Devil's Backbone Bar?

Michael McGar
Wimberly, Texas
April 2002

*Michael McGar's Profile:*

**Michael McGar** *attended Art Center College of Design and spent his next eleven years gaining national recognition as an illustrator. In 1989, his growing interest in multimedia led him to found and direct the Apple Multimedia Center in Plano, Texas, one of only three in the country. After five years in Plano, he went on to serve as President and Creative Director for Dallas based ArchiMedia Interactive. There his production, The Alamo "Victory or Death" with Sissy Spacek, Dan Rather and many other famous Texans, received numerous accolades including PC World's "One of the Years Best CDs in 1995." On the heels of this success, McGar struck out on his own, creating Alchemy Interactive, Inc. in June, 1996. As Owner and President of Alchemy, he combines his many years in advertising illus-*

*tration with his skill in interactive design to create unique, exciting interactive products.*

*Michael is a leader in interface design and digital media. His understanding of art, code and server technologies led to his invention of a new and powerful patent-pending internet protocol, which facilitates the creation of immersive Broadband experiences.*

*Michael also founded the Mid-West's only motion capture studio, creating high-end, special effects, optical motion capture for games, television and movies. In two short years, LocoMotion has become one of the premiere motion capture studios in the United States. Motion capture 3D animated figures will become as important to Broadband as they are to Playstation, CD games and, of course, the movies; LocoMotion just finished doing the motion capture for Spy Kids II, filming in Austin.*

# Part One

## The Power of Stories

*Chapter One*  **How the Mind Works**

Much of the time, an individual or team is not performing up to expectations because of a belief, attitude or perception that is an obstacle to achieving success. As the founder of three corporate training and development departments[1], my major objective was to determine how to teach individuals new skills as quickly and efficiently as possible, as well as how to change their attitudes about a variety of issues.

This chapter's conclusions come from my long-time fascination with the mind and how it operates and from many years of observing how people learn.

Many in the training profession believe that attitude problems result from a lack of skills and/or knowledge. They say poor attitudes exist because people don't clearly understand, at the expected level, what their job is or how to perform it—or both!

My experience has been that more often, especially with competent individuals, the root cause of behavior issues is attitude problems. While this may not be the case when people are placed in new jobs without receiving the support they need[2], my experience proves that changing attitude will change behavior.

Trainers know that changing attitude and belief is exponentially more difficult than changing behavior.

**It's much easier to teach people how to do something new than it is to convince them they need to look at things differently.**

Therein lies the problem.

---

[1] Mervyn's Department Stores, Atari Corporation, and Activision, Inc.
[2] See Blanchard's Leadership Styles for a complete explanation of how this works.

The years I spent considering this issue have resulted in a hypothesis as to how the mind works. The hypothesis will seem somewhat simplistic to those experts who have looked more deeply into the scientific principles behind the mind's operation; however, like any good hypothesis, it explains things very well.

 **The subconscious controls what we perceive.**

The foundation of my hypothesis is that the mind is made up of two major areas, the conscious and the subconscious. The conscious mind is responsible for everything we are aware of; the subconscious handles everything else and is completely responsible for what we perceive. This is the critical part: the subconscious controls what we perceive.

The five senses[3] don't filter out anything. They don't have the capability of filtering anything; they are only capable of receiving data and passing it on to your brain. Due to the sheer volume, it is literally impossible for the conscious mind to handle all of the sensory data it is continually receiving.

Imagine what it would be like if the subconscious mind didn't filter out anything for the conscious mind? This may be what happens, at one level or another, with autistic children.

**The subconscious mind receives the data supplied by the senses, analyzes it to determine how critical it is, filters out that which is not critical, and brings critical information to the attention of the conscious mind.**

Statements from various experts that we use only ten percent of our brains and the conflict of this with current scientific understanding that "if we don't use it, we lose it" bothered me. If we've used only ten percent of our brain for

---

[3] The five senses are: hearing, touch, sight, taste, and smell.

tens of thousands of years, why does the whole brain still exist? Why hasn't it gotten ninety percent smaller? In fact, it has come to light that the brain is responsible for much more than had been previously thought; it has a job that truly boggles the imagination.

How does the subconscious decide what is critical and what isn't, what to filter out and what to allow to surface? I suspect there are many different reasons the subconscious decides to filter or not filter. I'm sure some reasons relate to the current focus of the conscious mind and others to survival of the individual.

Through dabbling in hypnosis, I gained some initial clues about the power of the subconscious to control perception, as well as how it decides what information to provide and what information to hold back.

## *Where's David?*

*As a high school student, I started hypnotizing anyone who would volunteer as a subject. Most of the time I would hypnotize people in the privacy of my own home; at times I would also do it, probably to show off, at school. This continued until the day I hypnotized a girl while her friend watched in silent horror. While I was putting her deeper and deeper into trance, her friend turned around, bolted out of the room and ran screaming down the halls of the school. Oh, well, the walls of the principal's office were not all that unfamiliar to me. I had to promise never to hypnotize anyone at school again.*

My favorite person to hypnotize was a close friend, Don Osborne[4]. Don was able to go so deeply into trance that I could hold a bottle of ammonia under his nose, telling him that it was perfume, without any adverse reaction from him whatsoever.

I remember one time when I hypnotized Don with some other friends present. Don was standing by our fireplace with his arm on the mantle while one of our friends, David, was sitting in my favorite chair. I said to Don, "Where's David gone? He was in that chair a minute ago."

Don replied. "I don't know. Maybe he went to the kitchen."

David, of course, was still sitting in the chair; because of his hypnotic trance and my suggestion, Don couldn't perceive him.

"Why don't you grab his chair while he's out of the room? He'll be surprised when he comes back," I suggested.

"Good idea!" he replied. Then he began to walk toward the chair, preparing to sit in it; but ... David was sitting there ... I couldn't wait to see what would happen.

At the last second, Don turned to me and said, "I need to use your bathroom." And off he went. When he returned, he went back to the fireplace and put his arm on the mantle.

"I thought you were going to grab the chair while David was out of the room," I reminded him.

"Oh, yea!" he replied and began again to move toward the chair. Just as he was about to sit down, he looked at me and asked, "Can I get a drink of water?"

"Sure," I replied.

When he returned, he again went back to the fireplace and assumed his typical position. I was never able to get him to sit in that chair.

---

[4] Don ultimately went on to become the Vice President of Sales for Coin Operated Games at the Atari Corporation, and one of the chief reasons for its phenomenal success.

So what happened? Why wouldn't Don sit in a chair that he believed was vacant? What stopped him each time he began to move in that direction?

His subconscious mind stopped him. That part of him knew David was in the chair, but was committed to what Don strongly believed to be true: that David was not in the chair. Don's subconscious mind handled the situation by taking his attention away from the chair, giving him something else to think about.

**The subconscious mind has a strong tendency not to allow us to perceive those things that would greatly threaten our current belief system.**

I am now convinced this is a critical survival characteristic. Most of us agree that to succeed we must believe, and often doubt results from failure. For this reason, the subconscious mind has a powerful tendency not to allow us to see what threatens our strong beliefs. It is a positive mutation that ultimately results in the survival of the  species, another example of the power of the subconscious to control perception.

## Where'd She Come From?

*As the operations manager of the Mervyn's Store in Mountain View, California, I often worked the Sunday shift. My MO (method of operation) on Sundays was to start the day with a store tour. My objective was to check coverage and thank everyone for coming. This particular Mervyn's was laid out somewhat differently from most. The major departments were in the center of the building, while the Boys Department and the Domestics Department were* on a wing of the building that took a bit of walking to get to. I had just finished saying hello and checking coverage for the main section, when I spotted the Domestics manager, "Jill ... didn't expect to see you in on Sunday."

"I had some work to get done on the floor, and Sunday's a great day to do it. By the way, I am alone this morning."

"No problem," I replied. "I'll make sure you get a break," and I walked toward my office.

Then I remembered I hadn't gone to the Boys Department yet. I thought, "I should go over to Boys and check their coverage ... no ... we never bring more than one person into Boys on Sundays."

I was about to continue walking to my office when I remembered I had two objectives for the morning tour: check coverage and thank everyone for coming in. I turned around and walked down to Boys to greet the person who would be working alone there.

As I entered the department, I saw Susan standing by the cash register. "Good morning, Susan ... I see you're alone here today."

At that moment, two things happened simultaneously. Now, it's hard to describe two things happening at the exact same moment ... so bear with me. I perceived a black curtain dropping down in front of my eyes ... and I heard an unexpected voice say, "Mr. Fregger!"

As I stood there for a moment or two in shocked silence, I perceived the black curtain rising; and standing there in front of me, right next to Susan, was Betty. Where'd she come from? She hadn't been there a few seconds ago!

I quickly recovered, smiled widely and said, "Betty, I didn't see you standing there ... just kidding, thought I'd start the day off with a laugh. Seriously, thanks for coming in today."

And then I went back to my office.

**"She hadn't been there a few seconds ago!"** Not true, she was there all along. What happened was that I was consciously *convinced* there was only one sales person in Boys; I *knew* there was only one person. Therefore, when I entered the department, my subconscious mind allowed me to perceive only one person standing there.

What is critical here is that I *knew* there was only one person in the department. If I had only *expected* to see one person, I would have seen both Susan and Betty right from the start. But it wasn't just an expectation; it was a firm belief ... there was only going to be one person in Boys, period. Because it was a strong belief, my subconscious was obligated to support that belief by not allowing me to see the second person. Weird, isn't it?

When Betty's voice broke through that perception, a curtain dropped over my current "reality" and then rose to show me the truth. It was an unusual experience to say the least, one that demonstrated dramatically the power of the subconscious to control perception.

In addition to everything else we've discussed, it appears that the mind is also categorizing and analyzing everything it receives; everything and anything that can be used whenever the subconscious deems it's necessary. This brings us to the discussion of intuition.

## It Works Like Human Intuition

In January of 1999, I became Chief Product Officer for Austin's Dryken Technologies, a data mining company with research offices in Knoxville, Tennessee. I was picked because I'm good at creating product, not because I'm expert in the area of data mining. In fact, when I took the job, I didn't have a clue what data mining was all about.

My first task was to get to Knoxville as soon as possible and have a long learning session with the data-mining scientists. The chief scientist, Dr. Nancy Grady, was still working at Oak Ridge National Labs at the time.

We sat down across from each other at the conference table and I said, "Nancy, you're going to have to start at the beginning. I don't know anything about data mining."

"No problem," she replied. "Basically it works like human intuition. Our mind takes in a tremendous amount of data continually; data about everything we experience, in every way we experience it. It categorizes the data and determines relationships of which we are not consciously aware. Then at the appropriate time, it feeds only specific, relevant information to us in the form of intuition. Data mining works the same way. The algorithms look at massive amounts of disparate data, determining relationships that could never be determined by human analysis; they report out those specific relationships."

I sat there in silence for a minute. If I understood what she was saying, this answered a multitude of questions I had entertained over the years. Finally, I looked over at her and said, "Let me tell you a story about myself; you tell me if it fits what you just described." She nodded to go ahead.

"As the manager of a men's store in San Jose, California, I developed a very interesting talent. I would watch a customer enter the store and walk toward me. I was usually standing in an area of the store about one hundred feet from the front door. When the customer reached me, I'd say, 'The Shoe Department is down that aisle to your right,' or 'Can I help you find a suit?' or 'Looking for a gift?'

"The customer would often look at me and say, 'How'd you know what I was looking for?'

"I couldn't answer ... I didn't know how I knew; I just seemed to know. I wasn't right all the time, but I was right often enough to make me wonder what was going on. Part of me wondered if an angel was standing beside me giving me this information, but I had trouble with this explanation. Angels must have more important things to do than tell me that Joe Blow is looking for the Shoe Department.

"I think you've finally given me the answer I've been looking for. From what you've said, it seems to me that from the moment the customer entered the store, my subconscious was categorizing and analyzing everything he did, where he looked, what he reached out and touched, how quickly he walked, what he was wearing, and on and on. It had done this hundreds of times as customer after customer entered the store and then made a request. At some point, through this natural data mining process, my subconscious figured out that people who behaved as this one was behaving usually were looking for the shoe department, or the suits, or for a gift ... whatever.

"Then I would receive an intuitive thought, a thought stimulated by my subconscious but determined by the data my senses had provided as the customer walked through the store to where I was standing. Right?"

"Right!" Nancy responded. "That's exactly what happened and exactly what data mining is all about. Our algorithms look at massive amounts of disparate information and discover, through the use of neural networks and other *advanced data mining technologies, relationships that cannot be determined in any other way."*

---

This was fascinating ... I sat down to learn about data mining and discovered invaluable information about the human mind and how it operates, what intuition is and how it works.

☛ **The subconscious mind "mines" the data it receives for unknown relationships and then delivers that information, at the appropriate time, to the conscious mind as realization, insight or intuition.**

So how does all of this relate to storytelling?

## Chapter Two — *How Stories Work*

Understanding how the mind works is the key to understanding how stories work to teach, inspire, and change beliefs, attitudes, and perceptions.

Essentially, stories work because they can speak directly to the subconscious mind.

In this chapter we'll explore how this happens. But first, a few reminders of how the subconscious mind works:

1) The subconscious mind receives the data supplied by our senses, analyzes it to determine how critical it is, filters out that which is not critical, and brings the critical data to the attention of our conscious mind.

2) The subconscious mind has a strong tendency to prevent conscious perception of things that threaten our current belief system.

3) The subconscious mind "mines" the data received for unknown relationships and then delivers that information, at the appropriate time, to the conscious mind as realization, insight, or intuition.

Even though the subconscious mind is in complete control of what we perceive, it gets its cues regarding what information to deliver and what to filter out from the conscious mind. It's almost as if we were saying to the subconscious, "Don't show me that stuff ... I don't want to see it!" The subconscious "hears" this command and then obeys, filtering out the information we would find disturbing.

It seems our subconscious and conscious minds have an extremely interesting interdependent relationship. The end result: We see what we want to see and are "blind" to the rest! But we've known that all along.

The problem is: how to get critical data into the subconscious without letting the conscious mind contaminate it, especially data that runs counter to what we strongly believe.

When we can accomplish this, the subconscious can then use the data as part of its analytical process and at the appropriate time, provide us with a realization, insight, or intuitive thought, potentially changing beliefs, attitudes, and perceptions.

One of the first times I became aware of this potential was in 1980 when, as the Director of Training and Development for the Atari Corporation, I looked at a system for changing attitudes called Neuro Linguistic Programming (NLP). My greatest understanding of NLP came during the time I worked with Robert Dilts[5], who even then was one of the disciplines most knowledgeable experts.

Richard Bandler and John Grinder developed NLP as a result of intense research into exactly how effective counselors changed attitudes and beliefs. Since interviewing the effective counselors didn't uncover the critical processes[6] which explained their successes, they videotaped both effective counselors and ineffective counselors in action. Then they analyzed the tapes to determine what the effective counselors did differently.

Once they had determined the differences between successful and unsuccessful counselors' behaviors, they taught those effective behaviors to the ineffective counselors and, as if by magic, they became significantly more effective. Their foundational book on NLP is titled *The Structure of*

---

[5] Robert Dilts and I worked together to gain a better understanding of the creative process by using techniques similar to what Bandler and Grinder had used to develop NLP. What we learned can be found in my book, *Get Things Done – Ten Secrets of Creating and Leading Exceptional Teams*.

[6] The effective counselors proved to be "unconsciously competent" or as Virginia Satir stated in her introduction to the book, " ... I was unaware of the specific elements that went into the transaction which made change possible."

*Magic*[7] because they couldn't explain how it worked, only that it did.

One of the major distinctions between the two groups of counselors, the difference that most interested me, was the way effective counselors used stories to make a point. It wasn't that they used stories, but how they used stories.

The effective counselors' storytelling process spoke directly to the subconscious, without the conscious mind being aware of what was going on. In other words, they were able to get data that ran counter to the conscious mind's current belief system—critical data—to the subconscious without it being contaminated by the conscious mind. Then the subconscious categorized and analyzed this new data, delivering the resulting new information to the conscious mind as breakthrough insight. This caused a change in the individual's attitude toward the specific situation.

Surprisingly, effective counselors did not explain their stories. In fact, in most cases, they went out of their way not to share why they were telling the client a particular story. When ineffective counselors told a story, they spent almost as much time explaining why they were telling it and what they wanted the client to learn from it, as they did in telling the story itself.[8]

If we understand how the conscious and subsconscious mind work together, we see why the effective counselors' stories had an impact and the ineffective counselors stories didn't. The ineffective counselors were begging, in fact, demanding the conscious mind to get involved. They were operating under the mistaken belief that the individual had to make a conscious decision to change. The truth seems to be exactly the opposite: an individual only changes his or her attitudes and beliefs through an uncon-

---

[7] Bandler and Grinder's concept of Neuro Linguistic Programming is best explained in their book *Frogs into Princes* (Real People Press).

[8] As mentioned in the Introduction, professional educators believe that we *must* explain the reason for the story and what we expect the child to learn from it.

scious process. Indeed, the process is much simpler and more reliable when it is unconscious.

The effective counselors intuitively kept the conscious mind out of the loop by *not* explaining. The new data, hidden in the story, was fed directly to the subconscious; the subconscious was then free to categorize and analyze it, making an uncontaminated decision about the value of the new data in the context of the situation confronting the individual. Once that decision was made, the information was delivered as a realization or new insight.

Through this process, the individual's attitude toward the situation was changed.

NLP isn't the only source that supports this supposition. For example, we know Jesus seldom, if ever, explained the parables. I wondered if He, too, understood this basic principle. So I emailed my son Jon, a Presbyterian minister, asking, "Are you aware of any times that Jesus explained a parable? If He didn't explain the parables, do you know why He didn't?"

## *Parable Proof*

*"Yes ... Jesus did explain one parable. It is found in Luke 8:4-15. I've included it here."*

**1 Soon afterwards he went on through cities and villages, proclaiming and bringing the good news of the kingdom of God. The twelve were with him,**
**2 as well as some women who had been cured of evil spirits and infirmities: Mary, called Magdalene, from whom seven demons had gone out,**
**3 and Joanna, the wife of Herod's steward Chuza, and Susanna, and many others, who provided for them out of their resources.**

*4 When a great crowd gathered and people from town after town came to him, he said in a parable:*
*5 "A sower went out to sow his seed; and as he sowed, some fell on the path and was trampled on, and the birds of the air ate it up.*
*6 Some fell on the rock; and as it grew up, it withered for lack of moisture.*
*7 Some fell among thorns, and the thorns grew with it and choked it.*
*8 Some fell into good soil, and when it grew, it produced a hundredfold." As he said this, he called out, "Let anyone with ears to hear listen!"*
*9 Then his disciples asked him what this parable meant.*
*10 He said, "To you it has been given to know the secrets of the kingdom of God; but to others I speak in parables, so that 'looking they may not perceive, and listening they may not understand.'*
*11 "Now the parable is this: The seed is the word of God.*
*12 The ones on the path are those who have heard; then the devil comes and takes away the word from their hearts, so that they may not believe and be saved.*
*13 The ones on the rock are those who, when they hear the word, receive it with joy. But these have no root; they believe only for a while and in a time of testing fall away.*
*14 As for what fell among the thorns, these are the ones who hear; but as they go on their way, they are choked by the cares and riches and pleasures of life, and their fruit does not mature.*
*15 But as for that in the good soil, these are the ones who, when they hear the word, hold it fast in an honest and good heart, and bear fruit with patient endurance.*

*16 "No one after lighting a lamp hides it under a jar, or puts it under a bed, but puts it on a lamp stand, so that those who enter may see the light.*
*17 For nothing is hidden that will not be disclosed, nor is anything secret that will not become known and come to light.*
*18 Then pay attention to how you listen; for to those who have, more will be given; and from those who do not have, even what they seem to have will be taken away."*

"*I think it is interesting that in verse 10 Jesus talks about why he uses parables. At the end of the verse Jesus is quoting,*"

**Luke 8:10**
*He said, 'To you it has been given to know the secrets of the kingdom of God; but to others I speak in parables, so that 'looking they may not perceive, and listening they may not understand.'"*

"*He is quoting from Isaiah 6:9-10.*"

**Isaiah 6 – 9**
*And he said, "Go and say to this people: 'Keep listening, but do not comprehend; keep looking, but do not understand.' 10 Make the mind of this people dull, and stop their ears, and shut their eyes, so that they may not look with their eyes, and listen with their ears, and comprehend with their minds, and turn and be healed."*

"*By quoting this passage Jesus is not just using the words; He is interested in using their meaning also. In Isaiah the people are made to be dumb on purpose. This is done so that the normal ways of gaining comprehension-- eyes, ears, mind--cannot be used. A different kind, or level, of understanding is needed. This "other" learning is needed so that the people may '... turn and be healed.'*

"Dad, what it is saying is that to experience real transformation ... the kind that turns your life around and brings about real healing ... it is best NOT to rely on our normal senses and ways of learning. It DOESN'T happen when we use our conscious minds ... but when we use the subconscious.

"A superficial reading of Luke 8:10 would lead one to think the parables were meant to be some code language only disciples could understand. To believe this would be completely WRONG.

"So ... in Luke and Isaiah we discover the general purpose of the parables and an explanation of the one parable."

---

**To achieve storytelling with impact: Don't explain why you're telling the story, and don't ask what was learned from it. Tell your story and then move on.**

If this principle has been understood for literally thousands of years, why isn't it more widely accepted? I believe the principle hasn't been accepted because we do not want to accept it. We want others to know we are trying to help them. We want verification that our efforts have produced the desired results. We want credit for what we have done.

## *Nobody Was Interested*

As the Founder of the Training and Development Department for Mervyn's Department Stores, I had the opportunity to attend every significant "train the trainer" workshop in the United States. However, one company I was very interested in didn't run a "train the trainer": Scientific Methods out of Austin, Texas. They did a program I liked titled *9/9 Management*.

I called and asked if I could spend a day or two with them discussing the program and the best way to get the concepts across. They agreed but warned me that I might be disappointed when I learned their training methods.

Their methods for teaching *9/9 Management* concepts were revolutionary. The leader of the session did very little training; it was set up so the participants did most of the training. The participants were provided the information they needed and then had to prepare presentations to give to the rest of the group.

"Most of us know that the teacher learns the most," I was told. "Well, we decided to take advantage of that fact and have the participants themselves be the teachers."

"Is it effective?" I asked.

"Extremely effective. People learn more and better when they do the teaching. In addition, they have a greater commitment to participating when the others are teaching. After all, everyone's in the same boat."

"If it works so well, why don't you teach it in a 'train the trainer?'"

"We did originally ... but ... nobody was interested. You know, when you get through with a traditional workshop, how affirming it is to have the participants come up afterward and tell you how great it was ... how great you were?"

*"Yeh. ... "*

*"Well, that doesn't happen after doing a workshop our way. Instead, the participants come up to you and tell you how great everyone else was. You, the leader, don't get any credit at all. Most trainers can't handle that."*[9]

It is difficult to work hard to do the right thing by others, and then not get any credit for your efforts. But that doesn't change the fact that this is how it works.

**When using stories to change attitudes and beliefs, your efforts will go unrecognized; you will not receive credit for your good work.**

---

[9] I ultimately designed a number of workshops using Scientific Methods methodology. These sessions are always very successful ... but they were right; I don't get the credit.

# Part Two

## *Entertaining Stories*

## Chapter Three — *Tall Tale of Turtles*

My wife Barbara loves turtles, as well as seeking after truth. I included this story just for her.

*At some time in the distant past, humanity forgot that the Earth hung in space and revolved around the Sun. The Masters of that time met together to develop an allegory to explain what was holding up the Earth. They decided to tell people the Earth rested on the back of a giant turtle.*

*As the ages went by, people forgot this was an allegory and later Masters taught it as a Truth. Then one day, a student came to one of the Master's with a question, "What, Master, is the turtle standing on?"*

*The Master thought for a moment and then said, "On the back of another giant turtle."*

*The student thanked the Master and went on his way. However, a week later, he was back, again asking, "Master, on what is the second giant turtle standing?"*

*The master again thought for a moment, and then replied, "On the back of another giant turtle."*

*Again the student went away, and again, he was back a week later. However, this time, before the student could even ask his question, the Master looked into his eyes and with a deep wisdom in his voice, said, "My son, it's turtles all the way down."*

*As the years passed, more and more students began to question the concept of "turtles all the way down." In fact, many of these questioning students became Masters themselves and found it hard to give this explanation to the students who approached them.*

*Finally a meeting of Masters was called, and it was decided the Turtle explanation would no longer suffice. They* would have to come up with another explanation to meet the demands of the students. After days of discussion and argument, they decided their story would be that God, after creating the Earth, had no place to set it; so He hung it in space, in the exact center of the universe. Therefore, the rest of creation revolved around it.

The Masters knew this was only a story they had made up to satisfy the curiosity of their students. But they also knew if they could satisfy their students' curiosity regarding where the Earth was, they could more quickly move them to the greater questions of what existence was and who they were.

As the years went by, even the Masters forgot they had made up the story; ultimately it, too, became a Truth all were expected to believe.

Then one day a student came to his Master and said, "Master, I have used some new instruments that have come into my possession and made some measurements. These measurements seem to show that the Earth is not in the center of the Universe ... what am I to make of this?"

And the Master said, "There is nothing that evil will not do to confuse us. These instruments are the product of an evil one who has given them to you to cast doubt on the Truth, to lead you from the true path. Take these instruments ten miles out to sea and toss them to the bottom of the ocean."

The student did as his Master commanded.

Don't worry ... there will be other students who will question what their teachers are telling them. When this happens enough, there will be another meeting of the Masters, and a new story will be written. This is the never-ending cycle of belief and discovery.

## Chapter Four  Danny's Story

**D**anny Thomas' ability to take a relatively long time telling a *very* funny story is legendary. He was one of the best standup comics the world has ever known.

But it is impossible to tell a story the way Danny did with the written word. Here's a story patterned after one of Danny's most famous tales. While not as funny as when Danny told it, it's a great story nevertheless.

### By the Light of the Silvery Moon

*A salesman was driving on a lonely country road in Iowa late one night. He was trying to get to Des Moines in time for some sleep before his first sales call the next morning, when he heard, and felt, his car's back left tire blow. Murphy's Law[10] had reared its ugly head.*

*A quick check verified his worst fear ... he was miles from a gas station with a flat tire and no jack. He stood up and looked down the road, trying to decide what to do. He couldn't see anything but the empty road and endless fields. He looked back the way he'd come and saw the same thing.*

*"Wait a minute," he thought, "isn't that a light way back there? Sure it is ... I remember passing that farmhouse! The farmer will surely loan me a jack."*

*His spirits rising, he set off back down the road toward the farmhouse with a spring in his step and a whistle on his lips. It was, after all, a brilliantly clear night with a beautiful silvery moon.*

---

[10] "Whatever can go wrong, will go wrong."

He'd gone about a mile (the farmhouse was at least four miles back) when he thought, "What if he's got a gun to protect himself and he mistakes me for a prowler?"

That stopped him in his tracks. He stood there for a moment or two and then thought, "Don't be silly. Prowlers would be sneaking around in the dark ... I'll just walk right up the driveway to the front door and knock or ring the bell in a very civilized manner. There's not going to be a problem. You need that jack, so get on with it." He started walking again ... but his step wasn't quite as springy and the whistle had left his lips.

He'd gone another mile, spending most of the time convincing himself that he wasn't in any danger from the farmer, when he thought, "What if he's asleep by the time I get there? What if I have to wake him? If he's mad, he'll never loan me a jack!"

He could see this would be a problem, and his pace slowed as he considered how he would handle it when the farmer appeared, angry and upset at being awakened so late at night. Finally, he thought, "I'll apologize for waking him and tell him the problem. He'll understand ... he's got to."

He walked for about another hundred yards; then with determination, he thought, "If he's upset, I'll explain how important it is that I get the flat fixed tonight. If that doesn't work ... I'll offer to pay him for his inconvenience. That should handle it."

Believing he had things under control, he picked up his pace again, feeling much better. There was plenty of light from the moon and by now he could even see the house, a ghostly image against the horizon.

He'd only gone a few hundred more yards when he thought, "It's wrong for someone to demand payment, to take advantage of another person in this way. If it was me and I lived way out here, I'd help people for nothing!"

He considered that line of thinking for a bit, and then went back to what seemed like a sure thing, "How much should I offer? How about five dollars? That seems like plenty but I am waking him awfully late ... and if the jack's in the barn, he'll have to get dressed and everything ... maybe ten dollars is better."

He walked on, with the house getting closer and closer. By now he could see there was still a light on in an upstairs window. "Maybe he's reading in bed or watching television," he thought, "Or it could be just a hall light, one that's on all night long."

Now he was getting real worried. "I'm going to offer him twenty dollars; he won't be able to turn that amount of money down. And ... if he's still angry ... well, I'll remind him of his duty to stranded motorists ... I've got to have that jack. I don't care how unreasonable or angry he is!"

With that thought, he walked into the farmhouse's driveway and right up to the front door. He couldn't find the bell, so he firmly knocked and waited for the farmer to answer.

Shortly he heard steps coming down the stairs, and then the door opened. There in front of him stood the farmer, with a smile on his face and nothing on but a pair of jeans. "Can I help you?" he asked pleasantly.

"What right do you have to charge me twenty dollars for borrowing a jack?" he demanded. "Well, buster, you can just keep your dumb jack!" And with that, he turned abruptly and walked briskly away, toward the next farmhouse he could see in the distance.

"That farmer will help me, I know he will," he thought.

---

Something remarkably similar happened to me one time when I was trying to help an angry customer.

He stormed into the store, demanded to see the manager, and then excitedly described his issue to me. When he was finished, he looked at me and said with determination, "You'd better take care of me or you will be extremely sorry!"

"What if I give you your money back?" I asked.

"I told you, if you don't take care of me ... you'll never hear the end of it!"

"Is it satisfactory if I give you your money back?" I asked again.

"I told you, you'd better take care of me!" He wasn't listening, that was obvious.

I had to get his attention, so I looked him directly in the eye and said in a commanding voice, "Pay close attention to what I'm saying. Nod if you're hearing me." He nodded. I continued, "Now listen carefully ... is it okay if I give you your money back?"

He blinked, nodded his head, and said, "Oh, yea ... that's fine." I handed him his money; he grabbed it and left, without so much as a thank you.

*Chapter Five*                       *Almost a Messiah*

When I was Director of Training for the Atari Corporation, responsible for all training and development programs at their facilities throughout the world, I visited one of our manufacturing facilities in Puerto Rico and stayed at the Holiday Inn in San Juan.

*I arrived at the Holiday Inn the night before my meeting, had dinner at the hotel, and took a short nap. About 10 p.m. I decided to go down to the hotel's "hot spot" and listen to the band while watching the locals dance to the music. The only seats available were at the bar, so I grabbed one and made myself comfortable.*

*It wasn't long before I noticed the woman sitting next to me looked very depressed. She was staring into her drink, oblivious to the world around her. It felt like she'd just lost a carload of loved ones in a terrible accident. As I thought about what might be wrong, it dawned on me to ask, " Would you like to talk about it?"*

*She looked up at me and said, "No!"*

*I smiled, shrugged my shoulders, and turned back to watch the dancing. A couple of minutes later I heard her say, "Yes."*

*I turned around, smiled and waited for her to begin talking. I didn't have to wait long. In a challenging, almost demanding voice, she asked, "Do all men walk around hotel rooms in their underwear?"*

*I didn't know quite what to say. From the tone of her voice, I knew better than to say the first thing that came to my mind, "No ... some walk around with nothing on." Instead, I didn't say anything but just waited for her to continue.*

She got a disgusted look on her face and said, "Well, I don't like it. It seems to me that he could have gotten dressed when he got up and not stripped down until we were ready to go to bed, especially since I told him how I felt about it!"

It turned out she had come down to San Juan with her boyfriend for a week's vacation. While they had been intimate prior to the trip, this was the first time they had stayed together overnight. Even though she was in her early thirties, she was fairly naive when it came to relating to a man on an intimate level for a full week.

After a fight over what was a proper way to act, the boyfriend decided he'd had enough and went home to New York City. She had the choice to either go with him or stay in Puerto Rico.

"I took a week's vacation, I paid for a week's vacation, and I'm not going to waste all of my time and money by returning home early," she exclaimed with vehemence.

She took a deep breath, looked at me with indignation and said, "And after all this, do you know what happened tonight?" I shook my head and started to say something encouraging, but she was on a roll and didn't even pause for a breath.

"I went out to dinner alone and found myself in a nice restaurant not far from here. The hostess seated me at a small table; as I was looking around, I noticed a man sitting at another table not far away. He looked like an American, but what really drew my attention was the bandage covering half of his head and his entire right ear. I found myself staring at him.

"After a couple of minutes he noticed me looking at him, smiled, got up and came over to my table. He asked if I was eating alone. I said I was, and that I liked it that way. He asked what it could hurt if we had dinner together, since we were both eating alone. He added, 'The worst that could happen would be having someone to talk to over dinner.' I *thought it over and decided he was right, so he joined me at my table."*

*At this point she started telling me all about this man she'd just shared dinner with. She told me his name, where he worked, why he was in Puerto Rico, and how he had hurt his head. In a few short minutes, I knew more about the bandaged stranger than I did about the woman sitting next to me talking her heart out.*

*Finally, she looked at me and said, "You know, I was actually having a good time. He seemed to be a nice person, and we were both from New York City. I even began to entertain the idea of going out together when we got back to the city. Then, as we were having our coffee and desert, do you know what he had the gall to say to me?"*

*I knew the question was rhetorical, so I just smiled and waited for her to tell me.*

*"He said, 'The doctor is afraid I might have a concussion and said it would be better if I didn't go to sleep tonight. Do you think you could come back to my hotel room and help me stay awake all night?' I told him he was crazy; I had no intention of going back with him to his hotel room for any reason.*

*"What is it with all of you men? Is there only one thing on your minds all of the time?"*

*I said, "I don't think all men try to pick up every attractive girl they come in contact with, but I'm afraid the percentage that do is fairly high."*

*She said, "I've had enough of that kind of thinking to last me for a long time. Thank you for listening; it's time for me to go back to my room."*

*I smiled, we said our goodbyes, and she left. I turned around to watch the dancing and quickly forgot all about her and the conversation.*

*The next day I went out to the plant and did my evaluation. I met the personnel manager, and he offered to take me out to dinner that night and show me "a little bit of the night life in San Juan."*

We met at the Holiday Inn around 6:30 p.m. He said, "This is Thursday night, isn't it?"

"Yes."

"On Thursday the hotel puts on a Get Acquainted Party downstairs. We can get some free drinks and maybe even win a prize or something. Would you like to give it a try?" he asked.

"Sure."

When we got to the party, there was a great booth available right up front. We sat down and waited for things to begin. A couple of minutes later I noticed this man coming through the door. He looked like an American, but what drew my attention to him was the bandage that covered half his head and his entire right ear. I couldn't resist the urge to stare.

He felt my eyes on him, came over to our booth, and asked us if he could sit down and join us. I said sure, put out my hand to shake his and introduced my associate and myself. He introduced himself and, with little surprise on my part (the bandage was a dead giveaway), I discovered he was indeed the same man who had dined with my lady friend the previous night.

We sat there for a minute or so waiting for things to get under way, and then I began holding my head and acting strange. They both looked at me, wondering what was going on. I told them, "This is kind of embarrassing."

Then they really began to get interested.

"Once in awhile, when I touch someone ... visions, like movies, will flow into my mind."

They began to show some discomfort. After all, the man with the bandage had just met me minutes before, and my associate had only made my acquaintance that morning.

I continued, "The problem is, when I have these visions I am compelled to share them with the people involved."

By then, they were looking at each other, wondering what they had gotten into.

"When I just shook your hand, I had one of these visions, and I need to tell you what I saw."

He looked at me, then back at my associate, as if to say, "What is going on?" and then back at me.

I continued, "I just saw you walking down a beach. ... I think it's early in the morning, maybe as early as 6 a.m. You have two cameras, one around your neck and you're taking pictures with the other. Two men with baseball bats come up behind you, hit you over the head, grab your cameras and bag, and run off. You struggle to your feet, make your way to the road where you flag down a taxi that takes you to the hospital."

I finished talking, glanced at both of them, got an embarrassed look on my face, and kind of shrugged my shoulders.

There was a moment of silence and the stranger said, "That is exactly what happened! How did you know?" I told him I wasn't sure how I knew, that the vision just came into my head when we shook hands.

I looked over at my friend to see a look of awe on his face. When I looked back at the stranger, I saw the same awe there. I knew at that moment in time these two men would follow me anywhere, would do whatever I asked of them. Suddenly I had become more than human—someone to follow, someone to lead them to the Promised Land.

We sat there for a while, in kind of an uncomfortable silence, and I said, "Does the name Peabody, Jones and Hatfield mean anything to you?" He said, "That's the company I work for! How do you know all of this about me?" I shrugged my shoulders and looked back toward the entertainment that had begun by now.

Over the next hour I slowly fed back to them all of the information I had learned about him from the woman in the bar. With each new piece of information, I assured my position in history as the new Messiah, with these two men as my first loyal disciples. Visions of greatness were dancing through my head; I knew someday millions would revere this hotel, the place where our new religion had first begun.

Then I said, "I see you having dinner last night with an attractive woman from New York City. The dinner is over and you are saying to her, 'The doctor is afraid I might have a concussion and told me it would be better if I didn't go to sleep tonight. Do you think you could come back to my hotel room and help me stay awake all night?' She gets angry with you, refuses to have anything to do with your plan, pays for her dinner, gets up and walks out of your life."

I watched his transformation as the truth flowed into his being. A smile spread across his face and he said, "You talked to her after I did, didn't you?"

I broke into uncontrollable laughter and nodded my head in the affirmative. He began to laugh, too, not only with the joke, but with the relief of a reasonable explanation for what had happened. My associate, too, was relieved. I don't think he liked the idea of doing business with a seer.

---

I had blown my chance at fame and immortality ... almost a messiah (sigh). I was sure I would never have as good a chance again. Or would I?

## Chapter Six
# This is Our Teacher

While I was managing a men's store in San Jose, I found that I didn't have enough to do; so I decided to teach retailing at the local adult education program. The most popular class I taught was Success in Small Business. It was designed for people who wanted to start their own small businesses. It was great fun and inspired a lot of people—some became quite successful.

During this time I was also very interested in nutrition. I had read nearly everything written on the subject and had actually become somewhat of an expert. I had also become friends with the curriculum coordinator for adult programs, Bob Hitchborn.

*Bob had his office at the school where I taught on Tuesday nights. One night I began bugging him about beginning a class in nutrition, and I kept it up even though he didn't seem to show much interest.*

*Finally he said to me, "Look, quit bugging me ... I tried a class on dietetics a couple of years ago, and it was a dismal failure."*

*"That was your problem. People aren't interested in that dry subject; they're interested in the kinds of things that Adele Davis and Carlton Fredericks are talking about: popular nutrition and the health food revolution."*

*"I'll think about it," he responded and that ended the conversation.*

*A couple of weeks later I got my first surprise. He told me his wife had been bugging him, too, and maybe we had the right idea. Would I help him find a teacher for the program? I said I'd look around.*

I was attending many talks on nutrition at the time, and within a couple of weeks I spotted a nutrition lecturer I thought would be terrific. He was from Santa Cruz, seemed very knowledgeable, and was a good speaker. The next Tuesday night I told Bob I thought I'd found his man.

The following Friday I decided to check him out one more time, and I asked Kathie[11] to come along with me. The lecture hall was fairly large; I would guess there were about 350 people there. We all waited patiently for the lecture to begin. Finally, from the rear of the room, we could hear some applause beginning; as we turned around, we saw him entering from the back and walking up the center aisle.

The applause was fairly heavy as he approached. All of a sudden he stopped, raised his hands toward the ceiling and said, "Silence, please. ... God is telling me about a new vitamin, one very important to our health."

I looked at Kathie and she looked at me. Her eyes asked, "What have you gotten me into?"

I'm thinking, "I've got to get back to Bob and tell him I haven't found his lecturer after all." This would never do for an accredited adult education program.

During this time the lecturer, with his face toward the ceiling, seemed to be listening intently to some instructions from above. Finally, he turned his attention back to the audience and said, "I've been told that further information will be given to me over the next couple of weeks." Then he proceeded to the stage at the front of the hall and gave an excellent lecture on various aspects of nutrition. He really did know what he was talking about.

When the lecture ended, he gave a little bow and the applause started up again. After a few seconds, he held up his hands for silence and said, "There is someone here tonight that is very special. He is a very old soul who has come to Earth to teach, and he has much to say to us."

---

[11] Kathie was my former wife.

*Kathie gave me her look again; I shrugged my shoulders. In the meantime the lecturer was coming down from the stage, holding his hands out in front of him, scanning the audience as if he was being drawn to the aura of this important person.*

*I looked around as he came toward us and thought, "Who's he searching for?" As I looked behind me, I felt a pair of hands come to rest on the top of my head; I turned back, and there he was standing next to me.*

*His hands were on my head! I glanced at Kathie and she looked horrified.*

*Then I heard him say, "This is the man I've been told about. This is our teacher!"*

*I didn't know what to do. I was embarrassed, and Kathie was, too. What happened next is a fog in my memory, but I do know we couldn't wait to get out of there.*

*The next Tuesday I told Bob to forget the guy I had mentioned the week before, and he said, "That's okay, I've found my lecturer."*

*"That's great. Who is it?" I asked and got my second surprise.*

*"You."*

*Me? I couldn't figure out what he was talking about. "My credential is limited to business courses. I can't teach a class in nutrition," I said.*

*"That isn't necessarily so. I can make an exception for an experiment; and if push comes to shove, I can say that your retail background will help the students shop more intelligently for healthy food. I'm under the impression that you know quite a lot about the subject. Am I wrong?"*

*"No, you're right ... (gulp)"*

*"Do you know anyone who knows nutrition any better than you?"*

*The truth was I didn't. I agreed to do the course.*

*"Great! I want the first class to begin next semester."*

*What had I set myself up for?*

*The class was designed to meet for two and a half hours once a week, for nine weeks. This meant I had to plan nine lectures on nutrition and provide notes for students to aid them in their studies. We didn't have any idea how many people might attend. The last experiment (dietetics) ended the first night with only two students. Our hope was that we would have enough people to make the course happen— at least fifteen.*

*I came to school that first night wondering if I was doing the right thing, and whether or not anyone would bother to come. When I reached my classroom, there was a sign on the door saying the class had been moved—please come to the office. I walked to the office, thinking I was probably getting a smaller classroom. Instead, to my amazement, over eighty people had signed up; they had moved me to the auditorium, the only room big enough for a group that size.*

*Getting up before eighty plus students that first night was frightening. But as soon as I got started, all of the fear went away. I was talking about one of my favorite subjects before a group of interested people. I had a ball and couldn't wait for the second class.*

*On the morning of the second class, I got a call from Bob. He asked if I could come to a meeting an hour before class began. I was positive he was going to congratulate me on the beginning success of our little experiment. When I arrived at the meeting, there were a couple of people there I hadn't met before; and they all wore very serious looks on their faces. What had gone wrong?*

*It seems a registered dietitian who attended the first class heard me say my academic training did not relate to nutrition. She was incensed that I would be allowed to teach a class on the subject. She told them she was sure my lack of knowledge would be found out; she was going to bring authentic experts to each of the classes to prove how little I really knew. I had handed out the course outline, so* she knew in advance what subjects I would be talking about each week.

I looked at Bob, as much to say I told you so, and asked, "What are we going to do?"

"How do you feel about what she's planned?" he asked.

"It doesn't bother me, if that's what you're asking. I'd welcome that level of evaluation. However, I'll understand if you want to cancel," I replied.

"We're not interested in canceling. We want to stand behind our original decision. We just wanted to be sure you were confident enough to continue under the circumstances. If you're prepared to go ahead, so are we."

I will admit she tried everything she could to discredit me over the nine weeks. When I taught a class on milk and the differences between pasteurized and raw milk, she brought the state milk inspector to class. His letter to the district office said he had never heard a finer lecture on the subject, and he was glad he had attended.

The same thing happened with each and every expert she brought, until she finally called the state dietitians' association and complained. They had the editor of the professional journal call me to see what she was complaining about. The result was a two-hour conversation on nutritional philosophy, which resulted in an article recommending my class to dietitians in the area. It was a heady experience, one I enjoyed very much.

At the end of the nine weeks, I was asked if I wanted to teach the class again the next semester. It so happened, for personal reasons, I wouldn't be able to. There was actually a sigh of relief in the room. Bob quickly explained they were all glad things had gone so well, but the pressure of wondering what new challenge our antagonist might have in store was really too much for them. I said I understood and left knowing the class had been a success and would probably be carried on by someone else.

My one disappointment was never meeting my antagonist. She never had the courage to face me directly. I often *wondered, as I looked out over the large audience, just who she was.*

---

About ten years later, I ran into Bob at the grocery store. We talked for a while about the program, and he mentioned that the teacher who followed me was none other than the woman who had caused me all that trouble.

Bob said, "It was wonderful seeing her struggle with the questions from the class. She didn't have your knowledge of popular nutrition, and that's where the interest was."

Then he said, "You know, sponsoring that nutrition class of yours was the high point of my professional teaching career. That class modeled for me what education is really about: individuals, like you, sharing their knowledge with those who are interested in learning more. Thank you for making it possible."

**It was good to know that for him, too, all of the problems had been worth it.**

## Chapter Seven — *Hall of Fame*

This story is truly a mystery to me. Maybe someone out there can help me prove what I'm going to tell you really happened. It's very possible one of you has the proof sitting right there on your bookshelf.

*Sometime in the late seventies or early eighties, I found myself on a business trip near Canton, Ohio. Never a fanatic about football, I still couldn't pass up the opportunity to visit the Football Hall of Fame. I looked around at all the neat stuff on display, but I couldn't find the one thing I was most eager to see.*

*I'll never forget the moment: I was sitting at home watching the Jets play Denver. It was fourth down with the ball on the half-yard line; the punter, deep in his own end zone. The snap ... the punt ... the ball ... soaring over the head of the punt returner to finally touch ground at least twenty yards behind him. And it wasn't over yet, as the ball began to roll and roll and roll, finally coming to a stop on the half yard line at the other end of the field; officially, a punt of ninety-eight yards!*

*While I was interested in seeing the Hall of Fame, what I really wanted to see was a replay of that punt! Not only didn't they have a video replay, but I couldn't find mention of it anyplace in the Hall of Fame.*

*What's going on here? A guy punts a ball ninety-eight yards (really ninety-nine), and it's not important enough to make the Hall of Fame? In my opinion it was, and I was determined to make my opinion known.*

*I went up to the visitor information booth and asked, "Where is the display on the longest punt in history?"*

*"I don't think we have a display on the longest punt," the woman replied.*

*"Why not?"*

*"I'm not sure."*

*"Is there someone here who can tell me?" I asked.*

*"Maybe the librarian could help. The library is over there," and she pointed toward a door in the next room.*

*I thanked her, walked over to the door and knocked.*

*A man opened the door and asked, "May I help you?"*

*"I'm very interested in the longest punt in history, and I can't find anything about it."*

*"I think it was about eighty yards," he replied.*

*"No, it was ninety-eight yards. ... I'll never forget it. The Jets were playing Denver, and I think the punter was with the Jets."*

*"No way, there's never been a punt that long. I'm sure of that."*

*"You're wrong!" I said passionately.*

*He looked at me like I was a fan gone mad, turned, walked over and pulled a book off the shelf. He brought the book back, and I could see that it was the Official NFL Record Book. He opened it to longest punts and it said, "ninety-four yards, Joe Lintzenich, Chicago Bears vs. N.Y. Giants, Nov. 16, 1931."*

*"I don't care what the book says, it's wrong; that's all there is to it." He was discovering that I didn't give up easily.*

*In an exasperated tone he asked, "Did you say you thought the punter was with the Jets?"*

*"Yes! I'm pretty sure it was the Jets punting."*

*He walked back to the shelf and this time returned with what turned out to be the Official Jets Record Book. He opened it to the longest punts, and the longest was nowhere near ninety-eight yards.*

*"I still don't care what the book says; somebody's made a mistake."*

Realizing I wouldn't be happy until I'd seen every bit of evidence he could bring forward, he said, "You don't remember the exact year, but you think it was sometime in the late sixties or very early seventies, right?"

"Right!"

He went to the shelf again and this time brought back with him the Official Jet's Record Books for 1967 through 1971. He opened the '67 book ... not there. He opened the '68 book ... not there. He opened the '69 book ... and there it was:

"*Longest punt, 98 yards, Steve O'Neal, vs. Denver, Sept. 21, 1969*"

He looked at me, and I smiled at him with a look of vindication.

He opened the '70 book; it was the same as the '68 book.

"Looks like somebody used the 1968 book to produce the 1970 book and missed the new punting record," I said.

"Looks like it," he replied. "Thanks for stopping by."

What a great story I had to tell when I got home.

---

But ... there's more.

About fifteen years later I was flying back to San Jose and started chatting with the gentleman seated next to me. To my surprise, he was a past Director of the Football Hall of Fame.

"Have I got a story for you," I said with relish. And I proceeded to tell him of my experience at the Hall of Fame.

"It never happened," he said. "We always knew that Steve O'Neal had the record. There was never a mix-up."

"What are you talking about? I was there ... I'd never imagine an experience like that!"

I was confused. This guy seemed nice enough ... why would he lie about a thing like this? And if he wasn't lying, what happened?"

"I'll tell you what I'll do ... I've got some old books at home from the sixties and seventies. I'll send you copies of the relevant pages, and you'll see that there was never any confusion about who held the record."

He did send that information to me, and it sure seemed to verify what he was saying. However, that doesn't change or explain what I experienced on my visit to the Football Hall of Fame. It's a mystery to me.

While there's probably more than one explanation, the one I keep coming back to is this: When the error was discovered, they felt a need to not only correct the records going forward, but to also reprint all of the *Official Record Books* back to *1969*. In this way they could wipe out the error, even pretend it never happened.

There's also a chance that the guy at the Hall of Fame was playing a trick on me ... but I don't see how this could be. The books he had were official, and he handed them to me so I could see for myself that I was wrong.

---

If you have an Official Record Book for the NFL, for the years 1970 – 1980, check to see what the longest punt record is ... if it's not Steve O'Neal's, let me know. I'd love to know that my story was true ... that I really did correct the NFL record books.

**Email me:** *brad@1stworldlibrary.com*

*Chapter Eight*     ***Chihoe's Story***

Chihoe Hahn moved to Austin, Texas, after he sold his .COM, GolfClubTrader.com, to CBS Sportsline. We discovered we had the Silicon Valley in common. Moreover, my previous company's (Publishing International) law firm was the one mentioned in the story below ... that is why Chihoe first told me his story. I had to share it with you.

### How I, Chihoe Hahn, Personally Changed the Dress Code for All Attorneys in the U.S.

*Only in the most facetious manner could anyone, would anyone, so boldly assert (and open themselves to criticism from attorneys, no less) that they personally changed the dress code of the entire legal profession in America. So I won't, seriously. But to the extent that anyone would suggest such a causal relationship, I do. And I do so not because I really believe it; truth is, I'm not sure. Instead, I think it's one way of explaining how a real mass change occurred: casual dress becoming the norm for big firm attorneys. I'm sure there are other far-fetched, equally implausible ways of explaining this change. But this is the only version that paints me as a folk hero. So here's my story and I'm sticking to it.*

*The setting: mid 1990's and the day of the great technology IPO's and merger and acquisition deals. Every deal and every client was going to change the world, and you really believed it (at least I did). I was a third year corporate and securities attorney at one of the leading firms in Silicon Valley. (I won't name names so as not to embarrass such a respected firm for hiring someone who would write something like this.) I wouldn't say I was climbing the* ladder; it's more like I was a very small part of the ladder—like a fraction of a rung—working long hours and doing whatever it took to get deals done.

During those days, everyone was expanding, and fast. Our law firm was growing, too – so much so that by the time we moved into our brand new, dedicated, state-of-the-art firm building (most local firms shared office buildings with other tenants), the firm had already outgrown it. That meant – well, I don't know all the things that meant because I was only a lowly associate and wasn't privy to the partners' thoughts – but what it ultimately meant was that some attorneys and staff had to leave our great, new firm digs and go back to the old offices. There simply was not enough room. Someone had to be "annexed."

As you can imagine, no one wanted to go. Going to the annex would mean limited interaction with other members of the firm, no quick trips to the new gourmet cafeteria in the new building, and no easy access to the mail room for FEDEX cutoff or to WP (the word processing department and, incidentally, my vote for the title to Grisham's next novel). But still, someone had to go.

As fate would have it, the working group I was in was chosen to be annexed. On the upside, it would mean a larger office. But on the downside, it meant less integration with the rest of the firm -- a definite negative. The fallout from the decision to send our group "over" did lead, however, to an attempt by the firm to make us "whole" to the extent possible. That meant personal assurances that we would not suffer from a career standpoint; we would still be able to work with other attorneys on various important projects, and we would not be "forgotten" when it was time to make partner. This was very important for many of the others in my group; my perspective, however, was slightly different. Simply put, I was concerned primarily with the proposed perks.

Starbucks coffee was a start – back then it was still a novelty and seemed strong. Our own frozen yogurt machine helped as well. But, for me, the real selling point was the promise that we could dress casually so long as we weren't meeting with clients. What? No suit? I could tack the tie to the old corkboard unless venturing out of my large office? That was enough. Deal. We would go; provided, however, that the aforementioned perks would be delivered in a timely manner.

The first day there, we were greeted with a drawer full of gleaming foil Starbucks coffee packs, a new kitchen, nice big offices, frozen yogurt and the best view in town (a hint for you Silicon Valley aficionados). And we were dressed casually. ... Jason and I, that is (let's just call him Jason since that is his actual name). As it turned out, none of the other associates had come in that Monday in khakis or tieless. My first thought was that I had somehow messed up, and I would be reprimanded, socially and/or professionally. My annual review would start with, "Yeah, we said it would be casual, but you actually didn't wear a suit." Actually, casual dress had been going on informally (without a firm policy in place) for quite a while on Fridays. But this was a Monday. There we were, Jason and I, and not a suit betwixt or between us ... well, you get the picture.

After a few stares and "you're kidding me" looks from partners and associates, and some outright "you're not gonna make partner" cackles by certain associates with names like "Jon," I quickly ducked into my office. Later that Monday morning, Jason (who had worn jeans!) and I went into his office, shut the door, and proceeded to discuss this serious matter. We sat there, comfortably in our casual clothes, and agreed not to give in, not to break under the pressure. We would both unwaveringly dress casually because it was more comfortable and, more importantly, because that was the deal.

It must have been two weeks before the next associate came in, on a Monday, in khakis. Later that same week, another associate turned, and then another. The following *week, a partner without a tie appeared on the scene! Our "annex" was casual!*

*Word soon got out to the rest of the firm that we had gone casual. Firm wide, a few attorneys began to wear casual clothes on days other than Fridays. Soon, nearly everyone was casual. Next thing we knew, other firms in Silicon Valley, to stay competitive, were offering policies of casual dress. Soon after that, New York firms were going casual, etc., etc.*

*Now that the technology bubble has burst and the economy has slowed, firms are no longer doing everything they can to keep associates and continue growing. The leverage has probably changed, and I'm not sure what the dress code is currently.*

*In any case, that's my story of how I (well, okay, Jason and I) changed the dress code of lawyers across the country. Is it flawed or incomplete? Yes. "Scientifically" or logically proven? Not close. And, finally, for all of you bold, courageous rebels out there who are considering writing your own stories and building your own place in the legal or corporate world, and doing things your way, just know this: I left the firm shortly thereafter, and I would never have made partner in a million years.*

---

I believe strongly in what I call "casual professionalism." It is for this reason that I applaud Chihoe's efforts in this regard. Because he had the courage to see it through—he is one of my heroes.

*Chapter Nine*                         *Short Stories*

---

*I*n this chapter, you'll find several short stories, most of them true, told purely for your entertainment.

## *Customer Service Plus*

Mary was working the customer service desk at the Macy's Valley Fair Store in San Jose, California. This was not a pleasant duty, as happy customers seldom showed up there. But somebody had to do the job, and Mary was often the one chosen.

About ten o'clock in the morning, a gentleman walked up to the desk and began telling Mary the story of his refrigerator.

"You sold me a refrigerator that didn't work. Then you replaced it with another refrigerator that doesn't work. What are you going to do for me now?" he said impatiently.

"I can schedule a service man to come out to your house tomorrow to figure out what the problem is. If the problem is the refrigerator, we'll replace it right away with a new one," Mary replied.

"And what is my family supposed to do between now and when we finally have a refrigerator that works?" he fumed.

"I'm sorry about the inconvenience, sir. ... Tomorrow is really the best I can do. There's nobody available today."

Totally frustrated, the customer shouted, "I'll tell you what you can do ... you can take that damn refrigerator and shove it up your ass!"

To which Mary calmly replied, "I'm sorry, sir, but I can't do that. ... Another gentleman had me do that with a television set about half-an-hour ago."

The customer turned red, mumbled something, and left.

That afternoon Mary received a dozen roses with a note from the customer, apologizing for his behavior. He was a true gentleman after all ... even if his anger at the situation caused him to forget it momentarily.

## Where's My Suit?

When I was managing the Grodins Men's Store in Mountain View, California, it wasn't often I could hear an angry customer hollering all the way upstairs. But I sure could in this instance.

I got down to the main desk as quickly as I could and inquired, "Is there a problem here?"

A young executive type in his mid-thirties answered angrily, "You bet there is ... the incompetent staff you've got here can't find my suit, and I'm late for an appointment."

"Let me try ... I'm pretty good at finding lost suits," I said in a friendly way.

"You'd better be or you'll never see me ... or any of my friends ... in here again." He was not a happy camper.

I usually was very good at finding lost suits; however, this time even I was stumped. "This suit isn't anywhere in the store ... I'd bet on it!" I said to myself.

With that thought, I got an idea ... checked it out ... and discovered I was right.

I walked out to the front of the store, up to the angry young executive and said, "Found your suit."

"It's about time. Where is it? And when can I get it?"

I smiled broadly and replied, "It's at the Roos Atkins Men's Store at the other end of the mall, where you bought it. They've been waiting for you to pick it up. ... told me you were in a hurry to get it ... something about an important meeting."

He stood there in silence for a moment or two, then turned around and stomped out of the store, not even thanking me for finding his suit.

## *Percentage Error*

The CEO of Grodins had brought in a consultant to help determine if the stores were being run efficiently; that is, to make sure we were making all the sales we could make.

This particular consultant had convinced management that a good measure of whether or not this was happening was the relationship, percentage wise, between the two major departments: Suits (suits, sport coats and slacks) and Furnishings (everything else men wear).

If a store was running approximately sixty percent Furnishings and forty percent Suits, the store's management was probably doing an excellent job of getting the maximum out of each transaction.

When the CEO, with consultant in tow, got to the Mountain View store, we passed the store tour with flying colors. This was frustrating for the CEO who liked to find things wrong, but he held his tongue and deferred to the consultant for the conversation regarding percentage of sales.

Our percentages turned out about as perfect as they could be. The consultant told me, "You're running almost exactly sixty/forty ... keep up the good work."

That did it. ... The CEO couldn't stand it any longer. He walked over to us and said, "I'll take over from here." Then he looked me in the eye and continued, "Brad, you're doing a good job and your percentages look good. Now, what I want you to do is maintain the sixty percent Furnishings sales, but increase your Suit sales to forty-five percent."

I was silent.

"Do you understand what I want you to do?" he asked.

I quickly found my voice, and with my usual lack of diplomacy, I answered, "That isn't possible."

"What do you mean, it isn't possible?" he stammered.

"With percentages the total always has to be one hundred. If you increase Suits to forty-five percent, you have to decrease Furnishings to fifty-five percent. That's just the way it works," I replied.

The CEO turned and looked to the consultant for confirmation. The consultant was busy digging himself a hole to climb into.

### Daddy's Very Busy

I called Barry, a friend of mine, at his home. The phone rang a couple of times before it was answered by Barry's daughter, Jill, who was about five years old.

"Hello. ... This is Jill. ... Who are you?"

"This is Brad, Jill. Can I talk to your daddy?"

"Oh, no. ... He's very busy."

Not willing to give up that easily, I asked, "How 'bout your mommy? ... Can she come to the phone?"

"Oh, no. ... She's very busy, too."

"Is there a problem, Jill? What are your mommy and daddy doing?"

"They're talking to the policeman," she replied.

"Why are they talking to the police?" I asked with concern.

"They lost something real important, and the police are going to help them find it," she answered.

"What did they lose, Jill?"

"Me!" she giggled.

That didn't really happen to me ... but it's sure a lot of fun to pretend it did.

## Is that Seat Taken?

Judy worked in the payroll department of a major medical center in San Jose, California. There were two clerks working in the department ... well, let's say there were two clerks employed in the department, but Judy was doing ninety percent of the work.

She had put up with this situation for a year, having been told time and again by her manager, Bob, that the problem would be straightened out. After a year of empty promises, she gave her notice.

At the next management meeting, Bob explained what had happened," ... so Judy is leaving and I'm left with Patty."

"I thought Judy was doing the lion's share of the work?" one of the other managers said.

"She was. ... That's what makes it so difficult. In addition, it's why she's leaving. If I had dealt with the situation when I should have, she wouldn't be leaving, " Bob replied.

At this point, Jim, another manager, interrupted, "Sounds like what happened to me in London last year."

He had their attention, so he continued, "I was running for the underground, that's what they call the subway in England, when I tripped and fell down the last five or six steps. I got to my feet right away, but it turned out that I'd hurt my right leg rather badly.

"I didn't want to cause any trouble, so I limped over to the underground and got on board. All of the seats were taken in the car I entered, so I struggled to the next car where I found that all the seats were taken there, too. Then I saw a woman with her little dog sitting on the seat next to her.

"I limped over to her and said, 'Would you please hold your dog on your lap so I can sit down?' She ignored me, so I repeated myself in a louder voice.

"She looked up at me and said haughtily, 'Don't you raise your voice to me, young man. And you may not have my dog's seat.'

"I was shocked by her attitude but decided not to press the point. I'd surely get a seat at the next stop. However, the pain was so great I couldn't focus on anything else. When I next looked up, it was just in time to see the last seat being taken once again.

"By now I was desperate, so I approached the woman one more time, pleading with her, 'Ma'am, I've just hurt my leg and I really need to sit down. Please, may I have your dog's seat?'

"'Young man, I told you that is my dog's seat, and that's final!'

"That pushed me over the edge. Going a little crazy, I picked up the lady's dog and threw it out the window.

"From across the aisle I heard, 'Tsk, tsk, tsk.'

"'What?' I said as I turned toward the man making the noise.

"'It's you Americans ... you eat with the fork in the wrong hand ... you drive on the wrong side of the street ... and now, you've thrown the wrong bitch out the window.'"

---

Thanks to my friend Judy for sharing this story. I've changed the names to protect the guilty.

# Part Three

## Inspirational Stories

*Chapter Ten*  *One Shovel Full*

It is often said our children are our teachers. I was about to get a huge lesson.

We purchased our first home (San Jose, California) in January of 1970. It was a new house we bought for about $28,000 (which seemed like a fortune at the time). We were very excited about fixing it up, making it our home. After the rainy season was over, we started on the backyard.

We had purchased a truckload of beautiful used bricks that had been part of an old brick works chimney recently torn down to make room for more houses. The bricks were over one hundred years old, and we were excited about having some local history as a part of our landscaping.

As a child I used to go to that brick works and stand looking up at the chimney. It seemed to go all the way to heaven. It was the tallest chimney I had ever seen, and now we would have some of those very bricks in our own backyard.

Once we had the bricks and a plan of how to use them—a small brick patio outside our bedroom and a retaining wall across most of the backyard—we quickly figured out we were going to need a lot of sand to complete the job.

About ten miles from our home was a large sand quarry. So early one morning the kids and I hopped in the car and drove out to buy some sand. When we got to the quarry, I saw the dispatcher's office (actually a shack) on the far side of a small parking lot. I parked next to it and went inside, leaving the kids in the car.

The dispatcher was an older guy with a friendly grin. "What can I do for you? Lost? Need directions?" he said as I entered the office.

"No, we're okay," I gestured out the office door to my car with my three kids sitting patiently inside. "We were wondering if we could buy some sand?"

He looked at me like I was crazy. "Only if you want enough to fill one of my dump trucks."

At this precise moment another man walked into the office, smiled and said to the dispatcher, "There's nothing for me to do here today, Bob. I'll check back with you tomorrow."

The dispatcher looked at him, then back at me--and a light went on in his head.

"Joe ... how'd you feel about taking a load of sand by this guy's house on your way home?

"Where do you live?" Joe asked.

"Near the corner of Blossom Hill and Cottle ... about ten miles from here."

"No problem."

"Wow! Thanks a lot!" I turned to Bob and asked, "How much do I owe you?"

"You can have the sand ... consider it a gift. Ask Joe what he wants for delivering it."

I looked over at Joe.

"Got a spare six-pack?" he asked.

"Sure!" This was working out just great.

Bob reached for his mike, "Sam, you there?"

"Yep."

"Would you bring a shovel full up here and drop it in Joe's pickup?"

"I'm on my way."

Within a couple of minutes, the biggest earthmover I ever saw came around the corner from the quarry. The tires alone were twice as tall as our car. I could see the kids (Jeff, nine; Jon, six; and Bryn, three) pointing out the window, saucer-eyed, like me. Attached to the earthmover was a scoop so big it could have held Joe's truck with room to spare. And Joe's truck was the largest pickup I'd ever seen.

The scoop was only half full, but it held enough sand to fill the truck, enough sand to fill our driveway.

Sam drove that monster machine like he was part of it. Before I knew it, he was next to the truck, dumping his load. Wham, bam, thank you, Sam! I don't think he spilled a drop on the ground. I stood there in awe and watched as the truck bounced up and down on its shock absorbers a couple of times.

Joe hopped into his truck and hollered, "Lead the way!"

That snapped me into action. I jumped into our station wagon, started it up and quickly shifted into gear. We headed home, with Joe following, carrying all the sand I needed to finish up the backyard.

When we got home, I ran into the house, found Kathie and said excitedly, "Can you run over to the store? I just got a pickup full of sand for the price of a six-pack!"

"How'd that happen?" she asked.

"I'll tell you later. Right now I have to help Joe unload his pickup."

I grabbed a couple of shovels, and Kathie left for the store. She got back just as we were finishing. Joe drove off with his beer, and Kathie and I stood there looking at a pile of sand that really did fill our driveway. Then the realization of what I had done hit me. I was working the swing shift—I was due at work in just over an hour at 11:30 a.m.—how was I going to get this sand moved to the backyard?

"You know, all this sand has got to be moved to the backyard," Kathie echoed my thoughts.

"I know, but I have to go to work now and won't be home until late tonight. Tomorrow and Saturday I work all day. I think it will have to wait until Sunday."

"I don't like the idea of having this sand here for three days. What if it rains? Then we'll really have a mess."

"I don't like it either. But what are we going to do? I saw an opportunity to get the sand, and I jumped on it. Did I do the wrong thing?"

"No. ... but ..."

Then Jeff, who had been listening intently to our conversation, piped up, "I can move it to the backyard for you."

I looked at him and his nine-year-old body; he was a healthy kid but a little on the skinny side. He stood there in his blue shorts and tennis shoes, no shirt. His golden hair, bleached from the sun, was hanging down over his forehead.

He looked up at me expectantly, brown eyes wide with anticipation, waiting for my response. I looked over at the pile of sand and thought, "There's no way this kid can do this job." Then very quickly I realized that while he couldn't do the whole job, whatever he did move, I wouldn't have to. So I said, "Okay, I'll pay you three dollars for the job."

"You don't have to pay me, Dad," he responded.

"Let's make a contract. You finish the job, and I'll pay you three dollars. Okay?"

"Okay, it's a deal!" he said with youthful enthusiasm as we shook hands.

I went in and got ready for work. When I left home I noticed Jeff was already hard at it, using my smaller shovel to load the big construction wheelbarrow we had. I remember thinking he would have a problem handling it, especially when it was full of sand.

About 10:30 p.m. I arrived home from a long day and habitually drove into our driveway. As I got out of the car, I noticed the driveway was wet and wondered who had hosed it down. Then I remembered the sand ... it was all gone! Had Jeff moved all of that sand by himself?

As Kathie heard me come in the door, she looked up and exclaimed, "You're going to pay Jeff more than three dollars!"

"Did he move all of that sand by himself?"

"You bet he did! He worked like a trooper. He started before you left for work, and he worked straight through to dinner without stopping. I even had trouble getting him to stop for dinner. And it wasn't easy. He couldn't handle our wheelbarrow. But instead of giving up, he searched the neighborhood for a smaller one, going door to door. A lady down the street let him use her garden wheelbarrow. Then he had to navigate the construction we're doing on the side of the house. It was an obstacle course. It almost broke my heart every time he took a wheelbarrow full to the backyard. He finally finished at about 7:30 p.m. and still wouldn't come in until the driveway was hosed down. He told me, 'Dad won't be happy if he comes home and the driveway has sand on it.'"

I felt guilty. I hadn't believed in him, had doubted he would finish the job. That's why I had offered the money as an additional incentive. Now I felt cheap and small. But what was important was that Jeff had done it; he'd finished what he started. I was real proud of him.

The next morning I thanked him for all of his hard work and gave him a crisp ten dollar bill.

"Jeff, you did a terrific job! You earned the extra money. I'm proud of you."

"Gee, thanks Dad!" He was thrilled and obviously proud of himself, too.

"How did you do such a big job without any help?" I asked.

He looked up at me, hesitated for a second, and said matter-of-factly, **"One shovel full at a time."**

*Chapter Eleven* **Shanghai**

*S*hanghai has been on store shelves continuously, in various forms (none better than the original), since it was first introduced in the spring of 1986; there is not another computer game in the world that can make this claim. In addition, it is pervasive throughout Asia and has sold more copies at full retail than any other computer game. It was my great good fortune to be the producer who brought Brodie Lockard's masterpiece to the world.

### The Story of Shanghai

*One afternoon I got a call from Caretha Coleman, the wife of my boss, Ken Coleman. We often shared tips with each other on good people.*

*"Brad, you need to meet Brodie Lockard; he works over at Stanford University. I talked with him and was very impressed. I'd use him myself if I could get him away from Stanford, but there's slim hope of that."*

*She knew I often worked with creative programmers who had "day jobs," something she wasn't able to do.*

*I thanked her and then immediately called Brodie at work. We made arrangements to have breakfast together the next morning.*

*"We'll have to choose a restaurant that can handle my wheelchair," Brodie said.*

*"How about Stickney's at Town & Country Center in Palo Alto?"*

*"I've eaten there. That's perfect."*

*"8 a.m. too early?" I asked.*

*"I can be there," Brodie said.*

"See you tomorrow morning then." I hung up the phone and promptly forgot about it; I mean I forgot the appointment entirely.

I always keep my appointments (well, almost always). But this time I forgot and wasn't reminded of it until the next afternoon when I got a call from Brodie.

"Brad, did I get the day wrong? I was at Stickney's this morning until nine ... you never showed."

There was a long pause as I digested this. Had I really forgotten that appointment? You bet I had. I was very embarrassed. "Brodie, what can I say? I forgot. I don't know why, but I forgot. I'm sorry."

"It was a great inconvenience. It isn't easy for me to get out that early. I don't like to do it for nothing."

He wasn't going to let me off the hook easily, and I didn't blame him.

"I'm very embarrassed and honestly sorry. Is there something I could do to make up for it?"

Silence.

I continued, "Let me come and see you right now, drop what I'm doing and come right over. Will that work for you?"

Again silence.

Finally he said, "I guess that would work. How soon can you be here?"

"You're at Stanford University ... I can be there in twenty minutes."

"Make it half an hour. I'll meet you in front of the Hoover library. Do you know where that is?"

"Sure do! See you in half an hour," and I was on my way.

I was there first this time and had a short wait before Brodie arrived. He was a bright, good-looking young man about twenty-four years old. He had a large shock of blonde hair cut in a casual style that reflected the Stanford surroundings. He had told me he needed a restaurant that could handle his wheelchair. What he didn't say was that he was a quadriplegic. Later I learned he had been a Stanford athlete until he broke his neck on the trampoline.

Brodie took his circumstances in stride. In the beginning I had a problem doing the same, especially when I instinctively held out my hand to shake his. It was obvious this was something he couldn't do, and I felt embarrassed for not realizing it.

Brodie and I liked each other immediately. We had a wonderful conversation, talking mostly about learning (educational) software and a few other things. But it didn't look like we were going to be able to work together.

At the end of the conversation, I told him, "If you ever have an idea for a game, please give me a call first. I'd love to take a look at it, maybe even publish it for you."

About six months later, on December 17th, 1984, Brodie called.

"Brad, this is Brodie Lockard. Do you remember me?"

"Of course, what's up?"

"I have a game I want to show you."

Oh, no! Not another game, programmed at home in somebody's spare time. I had seen hundreds of these, but there were none so far I wanted to take to market. Moreover, I was busy getting ready for the Consumer Electronics Show in Las Vegas. But my curiosity got the better of me, plus there was the residual embarrassment of the original missed meeting.

The only free time I had until the middle of January was Christmas Eve morning; that was fine with Brodie.

So Christmas Eve morning I drove over to Brodie's house in Redwood City and was warmly received by his mother Dorothy. She took me into the living room where Brodie was waiting for me. He was in his wheelchair next to a table that held his Macintosh. But the Mac wasn't facing Brodie; it was facing the center of the room. On a coffee table in front of Brodie was a stack of tiles. I took the chair set aside for me.

Brodie asked, "Do you know what these tiles are?"

"Mahjong tiles," I answered.

Mahjong tiles are about the same size and shape as dominoes. The best are made of ivory and have very beautiful designs cut into them. With them you usually play a four-player game called Mahjong, which is like a rummy card game. This game is very popular in the Far East and has also been popular here in America from time to time.

The tiles on Brodie's coffee table were stacked in an unusual way. He explained that it was the opening stack for an ancient solitaire game called The Turtle, invented in China a few hundred years ago.

The objective of the game was to remove all of the tiles from the stack, leaving an empty board. You had to remove the tiles according to a couple of simple rules. It was great fun, but setting up the stack each time you wanted to play was a real hassle.

Brodie had programmed the game for the Macintosh. The computer built the stack each time, so the player didn't have to. And by using the Mac, he had created beautiful graphics on the tiles.

The Turtle appealed to me immediately. The game was simple but wonderful, a compelling and challenging game people would probably want to play again and again. I said as much to Brodie.

Now I was going to have to see how good the game really was. I'd be wasting my time if the game wasn't fun, fun for a lot of people. To test the game, I needed to take a copy with me, but Brodie didn't like that idea.

"I don't know, ... I don't want to lose control. I've worked on this for a long time. I wouldn't like it if something happened and the code got out."

"It's hard to proceed without taking a good look. I can guarantee I will take personal responsibility for your program. I will know where every copy is, and I will get every copy back if we're not able to make a deal."

*Brodie looked over at his mom. I saw her shrug her shoulders. I imagined the conversation had gone something like,*
"What do you think?"
"I don't know. It's your decision."
*I waited while he thought it over.*
"You'll take personal responsibility?"
"I guarantee it."
*He finally agreed, as long as I would sign a simple non-disclosure.*
"Sure. Do you have it handy?"
"It will just take a minute to get it ready. Can you wait?" *I nodded.* "Mom, can you give me a hand?"

Dorothy came over and moved the computer so it was facing him. Then she picked up a rod of some kind with a mouthpiece on one end, which she put into his mouth. Brodie then bent over the computer and began using this rod, or stick, to press the keys. He brought up his word processor, opened the file he needed, and then began making the additions. He was using the mouth-stick and pressing one key at a time to accomplish everything.

At this moment, the immensity of his accomplishment hit me. He had developed The Turtle in just this way—pressing one key at a time with a stick he held in his mouth. He had programmed the entire game, created all of the graphics, done it all ... one key press at a time. I was amazed.

Later I would see a picture of Brodie taken before his accident. He was in position on the parallel bars, his form perfect and his body healthy. I felt sadness that he couldn't have always been that way, but I didn't feel pity. Brodie didn't allow pity. He had programmed The Turtle as therapy. He had accepted this unexpected, unwelcome turn of events, accepted the facts of what he could no longer do, and set about discovering what he could do.

*The first person I showed The Turtle to was my wife Kathie. She didn't like computer games, so I thought she'd be a good test. If she showed any interest at all, it would be worth further exploration. Kathie saw the program for the first time Wednesday night, December 26th (I set up the Macintosh on our kitchen table). I showed her basically how it worked and then left to watch television and do some reading.*

*About 11 p.m. I told her I was going to bed. She said she'd be right there. I woke up during the night and noticed Kathie wasn't in bed. Looking at the clock, I saw it was 5 a.m.*

*I hollered out, "Kathie, are you there?"*
*From the kitchen, "Yes."*
*"Is everything okay?"*
*"Yes."*
*"Are you coming to bed?"*
*And she gave me, for the first time ever, an answer that would be heard millions of times around the world.*
*"I'll be there in a minute. I just want to play one more game."*
*I began to think we might have something.*
*The next morning I took the program into work and talked to an associate of mine, Sam Nelson. "This is a new program I'm thinking about licensing. Would you mind taking it home for the weekend? Maybe you could find some time to take a look at it."*
*"No problem, we're not doing anything else."*
*"This one's real confidential. Don't show it to anyone except Paula. I gave my personal guarantee."*
*"Gotcha."*
*On Monday morning, he came into my office and asked, "Can I borrow your Macintosh?"*
*"What's wrong with yours?"*
*"Paula wouldn't let me bring it to work. She wanted to play The Turtle some more. We didn't do anything all weekend but play that game!"*

*Now I knew we had something special.*

The contract negotiation turned out to be much tougher than I expected or it should have been. And it was my fault. I tended to side with the developer when it came to contracts, and I wanted Brodie to get everything I knew he deserved for bringing this wonderful program to the world. I negotiated with the company the best deal we had ever done with an outside developer. And then I went to see Brodie, sure he would be impressed by what I had accomplished on his behalf, and anxious to sign this wonderful contract.

But Brodie didn't know about my efforts, and he wasn't very happy with the concept of accepting the "first offer." What a mess! I had already pushed the company to the limit, and now our developer was saying it wasn't enough. Ultimately, Ken Coleman got involved and was able to add some considerations that made Brodie happy; but I learned my lesson and never again did I leave myself in a position from which I couldn't move.

We, Activision, had decided the game was good enough to move to other systems, so my next job was to find the people to do these other versions. The program looked so simple and really was simple. But the programmers I found, time after time, had problems duplicating Brodie's work on other computers. I had to fire the entire first group when, after three months, they still didn't have something playable on the screen.

This was when I first discovered scientific and business application programmers often don't have the skills necessary to program entertainment products at the level customers expect. Most "high level" programmers assume games are easy to do, but it turns out leading-edge games are an extremely difficult programming challenge, one only the top ten percent of PC programmers are up to.

Finally I got most of the programming started, only to have a problem with the marketing people. They tried to write the plan without playing the game. They wanted me to tell them what they needed to know. I put my foot down *and refused to talk to anyone who hadn't played The Turtle for at least half an hour. I didn't do management any favor; within a short time, we had a whole department addicted to the program, and lots of work wasn't getting done.*

*As you can imagine, I had strong feelings about the program; that included a strong opinion about what it should be called. I was in favor of Addiction. Since it was essentially a program for adults, not children, the name Addiction seemed perfect. But the industry had just finished another round of bashing by those people who were afraid we were losing a whole generation to the "addiction of computer games," so the company was reluctant to use that title. Ultimately the marketing team came up with the name <u>Shanghai</u>, and I learned why they were in marketing and I was in product development. The name <u>Shanghai</u> was perfect indeed. It spoke of being "captured," and it had an oriental flavor just like the game.*

*To my credit they did say in the advertising materials that <u>Shanghai</u> "was addicting," and that phrase did end up giving the product a lot of good free publicity. It worked just like I thought; the reviewers said things like, "Activision calls <u>Shanghai</u> addicting ... I doubted ... I was wrong. I haven't gotten any work done for three weeks. You have got to try <u>Shanghai</u> from Activision."*

*<u>Shanghai</u> has won almost every computer entertainment award given and become one of the most played computer games in the world, reportedly selling over ten million copies in all of its variations. I was happy, Brodie was happy, and our judgment about the kind of computer program people of all ages would enjoy was affirmed. And when industry experts talk about the lack of computer entertainment for women, they most often begin, "With the exception of <u>Shanghai</u>. ..."*

---

This story began over seventeen years ago, but *Shanghai* is still selling well around the world. This is unheard of in the computer games business, where extremely lucky games stay on the shelf only one year. This unequalled success is in spite of the many unauthorized versions available. For example, you may know the program as *Taipei* from Microsoft (this was the first of three of my programs Microsoft copied).

One of the reasons for the continued success of *Shanghai* is its appeal to boys and girls, men and women, of all ages and cultures. I moved to Austin, Texas, a couple of years ago. During the first couple of weeks a friend took me to Sixth Street, where all the action is, and then suggested we step into a tattooing and piercing salon.

"I bring my college sex education class here on a field trip once in awhile," she said.

My curiosity got the better of me, and I agreed. My first thought upon entering was, "I've got nothing in common with these people."

Then I noticed a black man behind the counter at the back of the store with more rings through him than I believed possible. He had rings in his ears, lips, nose, and even multiple rings in his eyebrows. Again the thought surfaced, "This guy and I have nothing in common." As I walked up to the counter, I noticed he was working at the computer. I said, "What are you doing?"

He looked up at me and answered, "Playing *Shanghai*."

---

All of this happened because a young man *seized the moment*, refused to accept defeat, and had the personal strength to rise above tremendous adversity. Brodie's commitment, courage, and ability to live with the facts of his life have been a continual inspiration to me.

I thank God for the day I met Brodie Lockard.

## Chapter Twelve  My Heroes

My inspiration often comes from those who have had the courage to challenge current beliefs, beliefs they can no longer support because of new discoveries they have made. Challenge an accepted theory if you want to be laughed at. Challenge a belief upon which a major structure of our scientific knowledge is built if you want to be hated.

The subconscious mind does not want us to see or hear anything that challenges our belief system. The more central the belief is to who we are, the more powerful our refusal to accept anything suggesting the belief may be wrong.

Below are three men who found the courage to fight the battle, to present alternative theories that, if true, would dramatically change our understanding of how things work.

**Immanuel Velikovsky** – The father of modern day catastrophism[12], he died a bitter man after his cruel treatment at the hands of the scientific elite. The value of his contributions is still underestimated.

**Dr. Louis A. Frank** – One of the world's foremost atmospheric physicists, he is still fighting to have his discovery of "small comets"[13] and their implication taken seriously.

**Eugene M. Shoemaker** – The father of astrogeology, Shoemaker is the man who proved that nature is throwing

---

[12] The theory that major changes are brought about by catastrophic events and are, therefore, not evolutionary in nature. For example, a comet colliding with the Earth and causing the extinction of the dinosaurs.

[13] Dr. Frank is at the University of Iowa. I won't be discussing his contributions in this book (although he is one of my heroes). However, if you want more information, here's the address to the "Small Comet" web site: http://smallcomets.physics.uiowa.edu/

rocks at us. Tragically, he died in an automobile accident in 1997. However, Shoemaker lived to see his theories accepted, with the final vindication being a phenomenal example of synchronicity.

These men are my heroes. They discovered things that seem to prove some of our most cherished beliefs are incorrect. Then they had the courage to present their views, even though their credibility was challenged and their reputations put at risk.

## *Immanuel Velikovsky*

*Velikovsky was a brilliant thinker whose concepts have not yet been, nor probably ever will be, accepted by the scientific community.*

*Of these three, Velikovsky easily suffered the greatest mistreatment. His reputation was literally destroyed by those who opposed him. Even today there are those who minimize his contributions.*

*I was blessed to meet Velikovsky and spend some personal time with him and his wife in 1973, when they came to Sunnyvale, California, for a speaking engagement sponsored by the Lockheed Management Association.*

*Every year the Association had a speaker series, and this particular year a good friend of mine, Terry Ross, was president of the Association. They decided to do a series on the "fringe sciences." As mainstream scientists and engineers, they believed they needed somebody who was familiar with the more esoteric disciplines. "I know just the man," Terry told them, and he gave me a call.*

*"What do you guys mean when you say the 'fringe sciences'?" I asked him.*

*"You know, the weird stuff ... like UFO's ... and other things that might be true but aren't accepted."*

"I could probably come up with a list and if you like my suggestions, I'll help you with the arrangements ... but I get to meet each speaker and be one of the hosts. Deal?" I asked.

"Deal," Terry responded.

So that's how I got the opportunity to meet and spend time with Immanuel Velikovsky.

It's hard to imagine now, but from the time of Darwin, right up until the late 1980's or early 1990's, scientists were convinced that all significant change was gradual and evolutionary in nature. The idea that cataclysm had any impact was not taken seriously, and anyone supporting the concept was believed to be a crackpot.

Velikovsky came to the concept through the back door. He was actually a psychoanalyst, one who had studied with Freud himself; and he wondered if societies and civilizations suffered from the same kinds of repressed memories individuals do. This led him to the hypothesis that perhaps the ancient myths of worldwide catastrophe, such as the great flood, might be true.

He set about trying to develop a theory that would support this hypothesis, one that could ultimately be tested. The result was his first book, <u>Worlds in Collision</u>. The story behind the difficulties he had publishing this book and the concerted effort scientists made to assure it would not be published in any venue giving it scientific credibility, is told elsewhere. However, suffice it to say, his reputation as a serious investigator was essentially destroyed.

What did he do that was so wrong? He challenged the absolute belief that the Earth was safe from cataclysm. Today we know, largely due to the work of Eugene Shoemaker, that we are anything but safe; that our entire civilization could disappear in the blink of an eye; that probably other human civilizations have been destroyed because worlds are, indeed, in collision.

Sure, Velikovsky's theories didn't describe the events and the results with complete accuracy. But this is what science is all about: coming up with a theory, trying to *prove it, and making adjustments when the proofs don't quite work out. Most of what he was suggesting couldn't be proved or disproved until others had done additional work. In the end, the foundations of his theory were proven to be correct: that cataclysm has played a major role not only in the history of the Earth and human civilization, but also that cataclysm comes either from outer space (<u>Worlds in Collision</u>) or from within the planetary sphere (<u>Earth in Upheaval</u>).*

*I call him the father of modern catastrophism because he brought this "new" concept to our attention.*

*When I met Velikovsky in the early seventies, he was very bitter about the way he had been treated. The sad thing is that his bitterness was hurting him more than it was hurting anyone else. I remember thinking after meeting him that it was too bad he was unable to celebrate those who supported him and embraced his ideas, rather than fixating on those who discounted him. But, to be fair to Velikovsky, the scientific community had been very cruel to him; he had good reason to be bitter.*

## Eugene M. Shoemaker

*Other thinkers, more fortunate, live to see their ideas, the ones that were once discounted, accepted and treated with the respect they deserve. Eugene Shoemaker was one of these lucky ones.*

*Shoemaker got his Ph.D in Geology from the California Institute of Technology (1947-1948). It wasn't long before he became convinced many of the volcanic structures he visited were actually impact craters caused by the collision of massive meteors, asteroids or comets with the Earth.*

*These theories were extremely controversial, flying in the face of the belief that nothing big could get to the Earth, that our atmosphere was our ultimate protection. Eventu-*

ally he and fellow scientist, E.C.T. Chao, provided the definitive work on basic impact cratering with the discovery of coesite (a high pressure form of silica created only during impacts). Now cratered sites could be searched for the presence of coesite, the discovery of which would identify it as an impact crater.

Later, Shoemaker was asked to head up all geological studies resulting from the Apollo Moon landings; the existence of coesite there proved that most (if not all) of the craters on the Moon were caused by impacts.

With the end of the Apollo program, Shoemaker shifted his attention to the existence of Earth-crossing asteroids; believing that they constituted a grave danger to our civilization, if not to the continued existence of humanity itself. In this effort he was joined by his wife Dorothy; together they have discovered more Earth-crossing asteroids than anyone else in history.

---

Even though Shoemaker did his definitive studies on impact cratering in 1960, many scientists still believed, as late as 1993, that worlds just didn't collide with enough force to cause any real damage ... that the chance of catastrophe was nonexistent. I told you at the start of this story that Shoemaker's ultimate proof came as a phenomenal example of synchronicity.

First, let's define our terms.

**Synchronicity is a cousin to coincidence:**

**Coincidence**: **Related events that happen by accident, the coming together of which usually results in a positive outcome for the involved individual or group.**

**Synchronicity**: **Related events that could not conceivably have happened by accident but which cannot be explained logically, the coming together**

of which usually results in a positive outcome for the involved individual or group.

So how does this relate to Eugene Shoemaker? Well, let's look at the facts:

1) Shoemaker was the first geologist to suggest that many of the craters we see were caused by the impact of a massive meteor, asteroid or comet.
2) Shoemaker suggested that these impacts have had a significant effect on the Earth, probably resulting in massive changes to our eco-system.
3) Shoemaker further suggested that the danger has not passed and that our civilization could be destroyed if it were to be hit by a big enough rock from outer space.
4) In the beginning, the scientific community refused to accept his theories, and even when they were proven to be correct, refused to accept that there was really any danger of cataclysm.
5) Proving or disproving this theory depended on the actual observance of a massive asteroid or comet striking a planetary body ... and what were the chances of that?

*Then on March 24, 1993, using the Schmidt telescope at Palomar Observatory near Los Angeles, California, a comet was discovered that was on a direct collision course with the planet Jupiter. What would happen when they collided?*

*Many scientists concluded we would never see the collision, believing the dense atmosphere of Jupiter would swallow the pieces of the comet like the ocean swallows grains of sand.*

*They were wrong. The pieces of the comet slammed into Jupiter with a force easily seen from the Hubble Space Telescope, and the pictures taken are a continual reminder of the cataclysm that would result should an asteroid the size of Gibraltar slam into the Earth.*

*Who discovered this comet?*

*The comet was named after its discoverers, the husband and wife scientific team of Carolyn S. and Eugene M. Shoemaker, and David H. Levy; and they were there to watch the pictures come in as the first pieces of Comet Shoemaker-Levy 9 struck Jupiter.*

*What are the chances that the man who proposed such an outlandish theory and then did the initial proof to demonstrate its truth, would also be the one to discover an instance of it happening and then be there to watch it take place? This extraordinary coincidence is made even more unbelievable when we realize this type of event is only supposed to happen once every few million years. This was truly a phenomenal example of synchronicity.*

---

Or ... as I like think about it ... an example of serendipitous synchronicity.

**<u>Serendipity</u>: The achieving of a significant goal that was different from the one originally planned for.**

The Shoemaker's weren't looking for deep space comets ... they were looking for Earth-crossing asteroids!

One of my favorite stories about Shoemaker I found in a short bio of him on the Internet. Mary Chapman, a woman who worked with him at the California Institute of Technology, wrote:

"*I remember a time when a newcomer to science overheard Gene's excited conversation and laughter at a meeting and remarked, 'Who is that loud guy?' – to which I replied, 'That is the 'god of planetary geology' and we all know that gods don't whisper.'"*

*Chapter Thirteen*  **The Garden of Eden**

While I like to think of myself as someone who is open to the unexpected and willing to embrace surprises, I have discovered there are times this isn't true.

*In the summer of 1981, Kathie, the kids and I drove from San Jose, California, to Phoenix, Arizona, so we could "caravan" with the Aldrich family from there to Jackson Hole and the Tetons. Two other families met us in Wyoming for this "extended family" vacation.*

*Diana Aldrich is one of those people who seems to have relatives in every state in the Union; this trip proved no exception. "We don't have to worry about a place to stay," Diana informed us. "I've got an aunt and uncle who live on the Navaho reservation south of Green River, New Mexico; they'd love to have us stay with them."*

*I wasn't sure I liked this, since I'm not fond of staying in strangers' houses ... but I didn't have much choice. To add insult to injury, even though we were traveling north, we had to turn due south when we got to Green River, driving twenty miles out of our way. I had trouble keeping my feelings to myself. In fact, I complained out loud numerous times until my daughter Bryn, tired of my grousing, said, "Daddy, don't be a poop!"*

*Just when it seemed like we were never going to get there, a beautiful rainbow appeared before us. This part of New Mexico was quite flat, but just to the left of us was a mesa with the rainbow encircling it. I pulled over, jumped out of the car, and snapped a picture.*

*Getting back into the car, I thought to myself, "Well, at least I got a great picture from this wild goose chase." It* never entered my mind that the rainbow's presence might be more than a moment to catch on film.

It turned out we were almost to our destination. About a half-mile up the road, we turned onto a narrow dirt road and up to the house where Diana's aunt and uncle lived. As we got out of the car, I thought, "What a desolate place. I can't believe these people have lived out here at the end of nowhere for twenty years."

Of course, Diana's relatives were beautiful people and even in my self-generated funk, I couldn't help but like them. After we said our hellos and got our things out of the car and into the rooms where we'd be staying, Diana's uncle said, "It's getting close to sunset. Why don't we go and watch it from the top of the mesa?"

I thought sarcastically, "From the top of the mesa ... yippee! If we were in San Francisco, we could be watching it from the Golden Gate Bridge or Half Moon Bay. Here we have to watch it from the top of some dumb mesa."

We all crowded into a couple of jeeps and made our way to a stopping point halfway up to the top of the mesa. "We'll have to walk the rest of the way," Diana's uncle explained.

When we finally did get to the top, we were rewarded with one of the most glorious sunsets I have ever seen. It had rained and the sky was still cloudy, but the sun had dropped low enough that it was shining its final light on the underbelly of the clouds. The colors were brilliant, all exquisite variations of a rich golden hue.

I took picture after picture, delighted to be photographing such a wondrous sight. Then I was interrupted when Kathie came to me and said, "Diana's aunt and uncle have something they want to show us."

"What could be more important than this gorgeous sunset?" I asked.

"Come on, don't be a spoilsport. They are our hosts, you know."

Grudgingly I went with her.

We walked up to the very top of the mesa and found everyone else standing around two holes that seemed to have been placed there when the mesa was just forming. They looked like the finger holes a child puts in a block of wet clay, except these were about two feet in diameter and four feet deep.

Diana's uncle starting talking as soon as we arrived, "In the Navaho religion there are five sacred mountains. If you look far to the West, you can see one of them, Ship Rock. This mesa is another one.

This place where we are standing right now is very special indeed, for this is where the Goddess of the Moon and the God of the Sun placed the very first two human beings. One was placed in this hole," and he pointed at the hole to his right, "and the other was placed in this one," and he pointed to the hole on his left.

Then it dawned on me: I was standing in the Garden of Eden! The Golden Gate Bridge didn't compare.

## Chapter Fourteen — Grandma's Poem

### *My Gifts to Keep*
*by Bryn Fregger Chernek*

*Tell me a story, parched paper and twine.*
*Of seeds in the window box, dreams*
*on the vine that grew through the ages,*
*then were,*
*then passed.*

*Save me the dew that clung to the blade,*
*opalesce jewel, till dawn dried to day.*
*The secrets of children,*
*sons, brothers now grown.*
*Of cup boards and pantries, the secrets of home.*

*Remember the color, for me, in his eyes.*
*A night that you danced,*
*a night that you cried.*
*The fragrance of clover and lemon and chive.*

*Forget not the fabric, the dresses,*
*their seams.*
*Forget not that blossoming basket of dreams.*

*And when,*
*at end,*
*that last breath sleeps.*
*Will these to me, my gifts to keep.*

*As always, your loving*
*granddaughter, Bryn*

My daughter Bryn was talking with my mother one day when the conversation turned to inheritance. For whatever reason, Mom was feeling a certain sadness that she didn't own things of real material value to be passed on to her grandchildren. Bryn assured her that the memories she so freely shared were of greater value than material objects.

As Bryn thought about it, a poem you've just read began to grow in her mind, one that said in verse exactly what she had been trying to say in person. She wrote that poem and gave it to her grandmother as a gift.

My brother Dennis was touched by Bryn's poem and believed others would also be touched. On a trip to New Zealand, he assured the poem would have a larger audience. This is his story of what happened on that trip.

## Set to Music

*In 1993 I was attending a Music Festival in Sydney, Australia, with my wife Pat and some members of the Santa Cruz, California Chorale. As I watched the different chorales and choirs parade on and off stage at the Sydney Opera House, I was completely blown away by the professionalism, excellence and extremely high quality of singing demonstrated by a group of high school girls from Auckland, New Zealand. The treble voice choir was lead by a gentleman, David Hamilton, who is now a full time composer.*

*After the performance I sought out David to thank him for his obvious contribution to the quality of life. Our time together was brief, and I assumed I would never see him again. But I knew I would always remember that performance.*

*After the Music Festival, we were on a plane to New Zealand, when a group of exuberant, energetic teenage girls* came bouncing onto the plane; and there was David Hamilton, shepherding them back home to New Zealand. I had the opportunity for a longer talk with David during the flight, and I found him to be a real gentleman.

When I visited New Zealand in 1994 with my son David, we had the immense pleasure to sit in on one of Hamilton's chorus classes (girls thirteen to eighteen); then we had lunch with him in the faculty lunchroom. During lunch I told David about Bryn's poem, and then sent it to him when I returned home. A few years later I discovered that David had, indeed, set it to music.

---

In 1998, New Zealand composer David Hamilton set *My Gifts to Keep* to music (for treble voice choirs); and furthermore, the Opus Choir (Auckland, New Zealand), conducted by David, performed it in Seattle, Washington, at a stop on their American tour. Bryn, who lives in Seattle, was an honored guest at the performance.

# Part Four

## Life Stories

## Chapter Fifteen                    *My Life*

**G**reg Walberg, a business associate and good friend, and I decided to start an audio book publishing company in 1994. Greg was also involved, as a major stockholder and board member, in Publishing International, our computer software publishing company. When we decided (after ten years) that it was time to shut down the software business, I was trying to figure out what to do next. I suggested to Greg that audio books had a great future, and probably because he loves them, Greg agreed.

I put together a business plan, and Parrot Audio Books was born.

*The business plan for Parrot Audio Books called for us to begin the company by recording abridgements of the classics. This would save us the hassle of trying to license current authors' works, as well as the money we would have to pay out as royalties. However, Greg wanted to do a Dean Koontz novel.*

*I didn't think Parrot Audio Books, as a new publisher, had a chance to get the audio book rights to an author of this caliber, but Greg convinced me that I should make the call to Koontz's agent.*

*The William Morris Agency is one of the largest talent agencies in the world; I don't mind telling you that I was more than a little intimidated calling them without an introduction. Usually it's best to get "someone who knows someone" to introduce you; but after exhausting my list of "someones," it was obvious that, in this instance, I was on my own.*

When I called, the receptionist immediately put me through to the woman in charge of audio book licensing, Laura Shapiro.

"Laura, my name is Brad Fregger, and I'm the publisher for Parrot Audio Books. We're a new company just getting started. Prior to this, I published computer entertainment software and shipped over a hundred products into the retail channel."

"And now you want to do audio books," she said. "I hope you know what you're getting into."

"Couldn't be any tougher than consumer software," I replied.

"Well, maybe not ... so why did you call the William Morris Agency?"

"Our major investor wants us to do a Dean Koontz book."

"You've got to be kidding! Even if his audio book licenses were available, I couldn't license them to a brand new publisher."

"Well ... thanks anyway ... it's been nice talking to you."

"And where do you think you're going?"

"I thought you just said we couldn't license a Dean Koontz title from you?"

"You can't, but he isn't our only author," she replied. "We do have other books available that I would consider licensing to you."

"You do?"

"For example, right now I'm looking for a publisher to do Burt Reynolds' and John Denver's autobiographies. The books will be released in the next couple of months. Do you think you might be interested?"

"Absolutely! But the author must read autobiographies."

"Of course, the contract includes that clause. However, it would be your responsibility to contact them and make the necessary arrangements."

The conversation continued for a while and then Laura said, "Send me a proposal. The terms you're offering sound good; I think we might be able to do a deal."

When I picked up the phone to make the call to the William Morris Agency, we were audio book publisher wannabe's. ... When I hung up the phone, we were Parrot Audio Books; and our first two books were going to be the autobiographies of Burt Reynolds and John Denver. To top it off, I loved those guys!

How could this happen to a brand-new publisher? At that time the audio book publishing industry was essentially two-tiered. On the top were publishers who were only interested in publishing the top-selling authors, and then there were about six independent publishers who were interested in other books.

Laura was in the process of determining which of these independents to license Burt's and John's books to, when I called. Somehow I made an impression; and when I offered the best terms, she decided to take a chance on us.

Within the month, David Shogren[14], our Director of Engineering, and I were in Jupiter, Florida, on our way to Burt's ranch. We could hardly believe it ... we were going to spend three days with Burt Reynolds recording the audio book version of his autobiography, <u>My Life</u>. Could things get any better?

I will admit we arrived at Burt's ranch with certain reservations about working with a superstar of his standing. We were quickly shown Burt's great personality when he welcomed us as if we were old friends. However, I still didn't breathe easy ... and wondered anxiously how the recording session would go.

---

[14] David was my cousin and he owned and ran a state of the art sound studio in San Jose, California; he was also a founding member of the Doobie Brothers. David passed away tragically a couple of years ago following a brief illness.

As Burt began reading, I soon had reason to feel anxious. He seemed uncomfortable and finally said, "I wouldn't use this word."

This surprised me. The cardinal rule of abridgement is, "don't add anything." I had abridged Burt's book myself because I wanted to take full responsibility for any problems resulting from the abridgment. Not only were there no words in the audio book version that did not appear in the book, but Burt had never communicated with me about the abridged version I had sent him a couple of weeks earlier. What was going on here?

"Burt, I didn't add anything. Everything you're reading was in your book," I responded.

At that point Burt blew up. He demanded to know what had happened to the book since he had sent it to his publisher. Nobody seemed to know; Burt had never seen a corrected copy. I felt sick inside. I had seen the corrected copy, and it was loaded with corrections. His agent went to check ... nothing could be done; the book had been printed, and Burt would be receiving his copies the very next day.

"It might be too late for the published book, but it's not too late for the audio book," I said. "Let's go through and make your corrections ... it should only take an hour or so."

"Good! Let me get my copy of the audio script; I have entered my corrections there." Burt left and returned in a couple of minutes. He handed me the copy I had sent him. I opened it, and inside were all the corrections. He'd read it after all. It took us less than half an hour to make all the changes in the computer ... now the audio book would be read as he had written it. The publisher's editing, in the main, had been poorly done. Words had been added for no good reason, and punch lines screwed up terribly.

After that, things went fine for the next couple of hours. Burt read, I produced and directed, the engineers engineered; and Burt's friends and associates looked on. There were about a dozen of us in the room. Then ... Burt exclaimed, looking right at me, "You took out the punch line!"

*The moment had arrived ... Burt had a major complaint with my abridging. "I know I did, Burt," I answered.*

*"You don't understand, YOU TOOK OUT THE PUNCH LINE!"*

*"I know I did, Burt. If you don't like how I abridged it ... put it back in."*

*Burt stopped for a minute, looked down at what he was reading, then glared right at me and said, "I'll read it the way you wrote it, you bastard!"*

*Let me explain what was happening here. When you produce an audio book, you can either do it unabridged or abridged. In my opinion, unabridged is the lazy way and makes no more sense than putting every word of the book into the movie. Audio is a different medium, in some ways more limited than the printed page. For example, you can't scan or easily go back and check something you've read before.*

*However, proper abridging takes care and sensitivity, and you usually have to cut a lot out. The average book needs to be abridged by thirty to fifty percent; I had to cut Burt's by a third. There were bound to be some disagreements.*

*There are two basic methods for abridging:*

1) *Cut entire sections where the end of the previous and the beginning of the next fit together seamlessly; or*
2) *Cut a character, and then the scenes containing that character come out like a string of pearls.*

*In this instance, I had cut a character ... but in cutting the character, I had also made a judgment that Burt's punch line, the one that included the character, was not, in fact, the real punch line. This is dangerous territory; abridgers need to be careful about their decisions. Burt knew what I had done, and he was rightfully upset.*

A little later we had a conversation and resolved the conflict. Burt wasn't happy, but he was willing to put it behind us.

The scene involved his audition with an important agent when he first came to Hollywood. He had recruited a fellow actor to do the scene with him. During the scene, right at the critical moment, the agent's phone rang. Burt saw that the agent was going to answer it ... he bounded over to the phone and yanked it out of the wall. Everyone was in shock.

Burt finished the scene ... then, "Nobody clapped or said thank you. Not a single word. They still hadn't recovered from the phone being yanked out of the wall. 'Screw you guys. Screw all of you Hollywood bastards,' I growled, and then stormed out the door."

This is where I chose to end Burt's story.

Burt went on in his book, "On the way out I heard, 'Oh, my name's Ed Thompson.'"

To Burt the joke was on him. The actor he had recruited was now in the driver's seat. But I had eliminated that character and a couple of scenes he was in; he didn't exist anymore. There was no way Burt could easily put him back in. In Burt's opinion, I had cut out the punch line.

A few hours later it started thundering badly, and we had to quit recording. During these spells, Burt would entertain the troops by telling Hollywood stories. I wanted to see the lightning and went outside. About ten minutes later I came back inside, and Burt was telling the group the story the way he had originally written it.

As I entered the room, Burt was saying, "'Screw you guys. Screw all of you Hollywood bastards,' I growled and then stormed out the door."

The laughter brought down the house. Then he continued, "On the way out I heard, 'Oh, my name's Ed Thompson.'"

Nothing but silence ... Burt looked down at his shoes, then up at the group and said, "I guess you had to be there."

Then he looked over at me and said, "I guess you were right."

From that moment on, we were a team, working together to produce an outstanding version of Burt's autobiography. He signed my personal copy of his audio book with this salutation, "To Brad, from the BEST PART of _My Life_. Burt Reynolds."

Later, during what turned out to be a disastrous book tour, I learned once more what a prince of a man Burt is.

Burt was very ill during the entire tour; this made it difficult for him to handle the ignorance and lack of sensitivity exhibited by many talk show hosts. He had been promised he would not have to discuss his recent divorce from Loni Anderson, about which he was extremely sensitive. Almost none of the talk show hosts lived up to that commitment, rationalizing that they had the right to ask Burt any questions they wanted.

Additionally, the tour schedule was grueling, and the publisher made little, if any, allowances for Burt's physical condition. The bottom line was that the publisher's representatives did a terrible job of providing the level of support Burt needed at this time.

By the time he got to San Francisco, he was obviously suffering from this combination of physical and mental torture. Then he ran into the worst talk show host of the bunch[15]. I ran into Burt immediately after the show, at a book signing at a local bookstore, A Clean Well-Lighted Place for Books.

I had not been told about the book signing by the book publisher, who saw me as competition. They assumed anyone purchasing the audio book would not purchase the book itself. To be fair, the book tour was on their nickel; anything I got from it would be gratis. Since I was not officially in-

---

[15] I won't give his name here ... I refuse to give him any publicity at all, even the small amount that might come from the publication of this book.

vited, I found myself in with the Burt fans, about thirty of them, in a section where we could easily watch the signing.

After I'd been there awhile, one of them turned to me and said, "So you're a fan, too?"

"Actually, I produced the audio book version of <u>My Life</u>," I replied.

It was obvious I wasn't believed. ... "If you're so important, why are you relegated to the sidelines?" was what the look on his face said.

Burt arrived, took his seat at the signing table, and the event began. Then I noticed Mike, one of the men who traveled with Burt, and I immediately went up to him. As I approached, he turned and saw me, "Brad, what are you doing here?"

"I live near here ... didn't want to miss the signing."

"Burt will want to see you; come with me." And he took me right up to the signing desk and said, "Burt, look who's here!"

Burt looked up, saw me and said, "Brad!" He then came out from behind the desk, walked over to me and, as he gave me a great big hug, said, "Sit next to me as I sign these books. We can talk ... it's the only chance I'll have ... I've got to catch a plane."

---

So I sat with him the whole time. We talked and he introduced me as his audio book publisher to many of the people who came by. Burt is a great man ... deserving of any and all awards and accolades that come to him.

*Chapter Sixteen*                          ***Fregger's Law***

About six weeks after recording Burt Reynolds, David and I went to Aspen, Colorado, to spend a couple of days with John Denver recording his autobiography, *Take Me Home.*

If you believe John Denver, the person, was a reflection of his songs, this story may disappoint you. However, if I'm going to tell my story, I need to tell it like it happened.[16]

*David and I were sitting in the San Francisco International Airport waiting to board our flight to Aspen. I looked over at him and he looked back; we both starting laughing.*

*"We spent three days last month with Burt at his ranch, and now we're on our way to Aspen to spend a couple of days working with John at his home," I said. "I'm having the time of my life; how about you?"*

*"This is great ... it really is," he replied.*

*"Have we got everything we need?" I asked.*

*"I didn't bring much. Burt's people told you we wouldn't need anything, and I brought it all anyway. This time I decided to trust."*

*Just as David said this, two things happened simultaneously: they announced boarding for our plane and my pager went off. I glanced at my pager and saw the number of John Denver's personal secretary.*

*"John's secretary is paging me; I'll be right back," I said anxiously as I ran for a nearby payphone.*

*Joan (I've changed her name) answered, we said our hellos, then she said, "Brad, I know I told you that John*

---

[16] To be fair, we got to Aspen only a couple of days after John had gotten out of a month of rehabilitation, so it's possible we didn't catch him at the best of times.

had a recording studio with all the equipment and supplies you would need. But he just told me he doesn't have anything, and you will have to bring your own stuff."

I didn't know what to say. This was not good news. We were already a month behind in our schedule because John had been in court-ordered rehabilitation. Now here we were at the airport, the boarding announcement already made, and she tells me we need all our equipment.

"Hold on a second; I need to talk to my engineer," I said.

"David!" I hollered out. He saw my concern and came right over. "Joan just told me they don't have any equipment. What are we going to do? And don't say reschedule; we can't afford to put it off. There's no telling when he'll be available again."

"I can make it work. We ought to be able to rent a machine or locate a sound studio."

I turned back to the phone and said, "We'll need to rent some equipment. What's the chance of finding it in Aspen?"

"That shouldn't be a problem ... there's two or three stores in town that handle all kinds of recording stuff," she replied.

"Okay, we're coming. We can't put it off any longer. I've got to go now; they've called for boarding. We'll see you in a few hours." I hung up and we ran for the plane.

Early that afternoon we drove up to John's house and parked in the driveway. John was in the garage working on his motorcycle. He looked up as we walked in.

"You guys here to record my book?" he asked.

"Yes, I'm Brad Fregger and this is David Shogren, our Director of Engineering. It's good to be here. I couldn't wait to meet you. Your music has always been very special to me."

"Thank you. Let's go in. I need to wash my hands, and then I'll show you around."

First impression ... John was just as great a guy as I thought he was, very personable and easy to talk to.

After he washed his hands, he took us on a tour of his home. When we got to the back of the house, he showed us into a room and said, "This is my recording studio."

"I'm confused ... your secretary called me just before we left and told me you didn't have a recording studio."

"What she meant to say was we wouldn't be able to use it," he replied. The tone of his voice said, "And don't try and change my mind." I decided to let it go.

Then we went to the family room, which was just off the kitchen. Joan was waiting for us.

As we entered John said, "Joan tells me you were going to rent some equipment when you got to town." I nodded.

He walked to the kitchen table and picked up a portable DAT (Digital Audio Tape) machine. "I've got this DAT recorder you can use, and I thought we could record out in the backyard. It's pretty quiet up here."

Joan added, "And I went shopping and bought up all the DAT tapes in town. I found eight ... will that be enough?"

I couldn't help but think back on the Burt Reynolds experience. Both personal secretaries had told me the same thing, "We have everything you need." But while Burt built a recording studio at his ranch just to record the book and brought in his own engineers to make sure everything was just the way he wanted it, John decided we couldn't use the studio he already had and was suggesting we record on a portable DAT machine in his backyard.

"Let's give it a try and see if we can make it work," I said.

"What I want to know," John said in an almost angry voice, "is why you guys would come all this way to record my book and not have the equipment, even the tape, you needed to do the job?"

This statement surprised me; surely he knew we had been led astray. I glanced at Joan, who was standing behind John, the look on her face imploring me, "Please don't tell him what happened."

I looked back at John and said, "I'm sorry, but with this equipment and the tapes Joan found, I'm sure we'll make do. Let's see where we can set up," and I walked out the door into the backyard.

John's home was north of Aspen, in the hills above the airport. We could see the planes landing and taking off and my first thought was, "Will those planes interfere with the recording?"

We finally settled on using the patio with its table and chairs. David rigged a mike stand, the computer sat on a rubber mat, and we did a test. Everything tested out fine ... the only thing we could hear was the wind blowing through the aspens in his yard. I liked the ambiance, so we began recording.

John was a great reader and the recording went smoothly. It looked like we were going to be able to finish up a day early. For such a bad beginning, things had worked out remarkably well.

We needed a second DAT machine, because we had to have copies of the tape ... I wasn't leaving Aspen with only one copy. We were able to rent the only available machine that first night.

We ended up having the exact number of tapes we needed to complete the job, running out of tape just as John finished the book.

The final omen that told me the trip had ended up a perfect one happened as we left on the plane. I had wanted a window seat badly, so I could see the Rocky Mountains as we left Aspen. I was told at the counter that the plane was full, and there were no window seats left. We had to take an aisle and center seat; at least we got to sit together. David and I flipped for the aisle seat and he won. We boarded the plane and when it took off, there was only one seat vacant ... the window seat next to me! I had a great view of the Rockies all the way to Denver.

However, there were a few other disappointments for me. First, on the morning of the second day, John had shown me his new Macintosh computer; and I offered to send him some of the Macintosh programs I had produced which were fairly well known (i.e. Shanghai, Solitaire Royale, Ishido, and Heaven & Earth). All told, I sent him more than $300 worth of games and applications ... all new.

One evening a week or so after I was back home, the phone rang. Kathie answered and handed it to me, "Brad, it's John Denver."

"John, what can I do for you?"

"I'm having trouble getting these programs you sent me installed. I need your help."

"No problem. ... " And I spent about an hour on the phone with him getting everything working right.

I didn't send him the software and then help him get it up and working just to be on his good side (I've done the same kind of thing for many others over the years). However, it did enter my mind that I might need his help sometime.

It wasn't long before I did. I needed two things: first, I needed recent pictures for the inside of the audio book packaging; and second, I needed a release to use about ten seconds of some of his songs as chapter breaks.

It was impossible to get either. "If you want them, get them from the record company," John said matter-of-factly.

I wanted the songs (only the first ten seconds) so I could make the audio book into something very special ... he didn't see it that way. He seemed to think I was trying to get something for nothing. His record company wouldn't give me permission either. I finally had to license the songs and have a local guitarist play snippets of each one for the book.[17]

And he wouldn't let me have any current pictures either. He insisted I go to his agent and get pictures that were

---

[17] Turns out you can use ten seconds of any song without permission, much like you can quote from any book as long as the quote isn't too long. It's too bad I didn't find out in time.

years old and not very flattering to him or Annie (his former wife).

Again I couldn't help comparing him to Burt. When I asked for a picture of Burt and his son, he promptly sent a nice recent one. However, it was vertical and I needed horizontal. I called back and had a horizontal version on my desk the next morning.

So John's audio book wasn't everything I had hoped for ... but it's still darn good, and the way things worked out on the recording trip was almost miraculous. It was the antithesis of Murphy's Law, "Everything that can go wrong, will go wrong." I call it Fregger's Principle:

**"Everything that can go right, will go right!"**

## Chapter Seventeen — *Solitaire*

*T*he Macintosh version of *Shanghai* was out almost three months before the IBM version. On the very day the IBM "ship decision" was made, I received an IBM disk in the mail from Mike Sandige, a sophomore at the University of Colorado in Boulder. I put the disk into my computer and up came a version of *Shanghai* that, in many ways, was better than the one we had just decided to ship.

His letter said in part, "I saw the Macintosh version in the computer software store I work in, and I liked it so much I took a month and put this IBM version together. My friends thought it was good enough to show you, that maybe you'd want to market it."

One month ... and I had spent the first three months just trying to find someone who could move it to the IBM! After our lawyers wrote Mike a letter stating very clearly that his version should not be distributed to anyone in any way, I decided to stay in touch with this young man who seemed to be so talented as a programmer. And that brings us to the story of computer card solitaire.

*I left Activision in September of 1985, so Kathie and I could start our own company, Publishing International, with our best friends, Dick and Diana Aldrich.*

*During the Christmas season my folks would come to visit us for a month or so, and this year wasn't any different. Dad loved to play cards, so it was a habit of ours to play cards almost every night.*

*On this particular night we were getting off to a late start because my Mother was playing Shanghai and wanted to complete the game she had going.*

Brad Fregger      One Shovel Full      121

*Impatiently, Dad asked, "Are we going to play cards tonight or not?"*

*"I thought we were," I replied. "We'll get started as soon as Mom's finished playing Shanghai."*

*"She's playing Shanghai?" he asked incredulously. "We'll never get started."*

*"She said she was just going to play one more game," I said with a grin.*

*Then he looked me directly in the eye, shook his finger at me, and with determination said, "I'll never be addicted to a computer game!"*

As we played cards that night, I couldn't get Dad's statement out of my mind. What a challenge ... could I do a computer game that would addict even him? What kind of a game would it have to be? Then I thought, "Dad likes to play cards ... he loves card solitaire ... what about computer card solitaire?"

The more I thought about it, the better it sounded. Computer card solitaire would actually have a lot of the same characteristics of Shanghai ... most importantly, you wouldn't have to shuffle before every game; the computer would shuffle and set up the game for you.

I was determined to put together an initial design and take it to a publisher, Spectrum Holobyte, that I believed would be interested in it.

For a design I used the games that were the favorites for our family, the ones we knew best. The eight games included were: Klondike, Canfield, Four Corners, Calculation, Three Shuffles & a Draw, Vegas, Pyramid, and Golf.

The first chance I had, I went to Spectrum Holobyte to see if I could convince them to publish computer card solitaire. After a short negotiation, Phil Adams, the president, said, "Nobody's going to play solitaire on the computer, not when they could reach into their desk drawer and pull out a deck of cards. This is risky ... I'll tell you what, you take the development risk and I'll take the publishing risk." Sneaky of him, since he knew I'd bite ... and he was right!

*Spectrum Holobyte named the game Solitaire Royale. Brodie Lockard (Shanghai) programmed the Macintosh version, while Mike Sandige (the college student from Boulder, Colorado) did the IBM version. My brother Dennis did the Macintosh graphics and, in my opinion, those graphics are still, seventeen years later, the best looking card graphics in the world.*

*Oh, yes ... Dad and Mom had to bring their own computer when they visited next. He was hooked on Solitaire Royale, and Mom ... well, she was hooked on both Solitaire Royale and Shanghai ... mission accomplished!*

---

Solitaire is the world's most played computer game, because, after Microsoft saw it, they decided to put a version of Klondike in Windows. Later, when they realized they had a phenomenally successful "demo," they contacted me and asked us to do the Microsoft computer card solitaire product. I learned the hard way that it's not a good idea to get in bed with Satan; the "relationship" almost bankrupt us. When our internal champion got promoted, the new guy refused to honor any of our agreements; we were never even notified.

By giving away a version of solitaire with Windows, they have the dubious honor of having created the most successful demo of all times while never producing the final product. They have also assured for me a place in computer entertainment software history.[18]

---

[18] There's a lot more to the Microsoft/Solitaire story ... you can read it all in my first book, "*Lucky That Way – Stories of Seizing the Moment While Creating the Games Millions Play*"

## Chapter Eighteen

# *Oh, Shit!*

We had been buying used or inexpensive cars for most of our married life, and I had always wanted to go into a showroom and purchase a real nice car. We ended up at the Oldsmobile dealership in Los Gatos, California, where I fell in love with a beautiful, copper-colored, small Olds sitting right in the center of the showroom floor.

*About six months later I was driving my still new, copper-colored Olds home from work one evening and had reached a stretch of freeway where typically the traffic slowed down just before my exit. That evening the traffic was slowing down sooner, just before an off-ramp I sometimes used when the traffic was particularly heavy.*

*As I came to a stop behind a small pickup, I glanced in the rearview mirror to see if it was safe to shoot down the off-ramp. What I saw behind me was a big tank of a Buick, bearing down on my rear bumper at about fifty miles an hour. It couldn't have been more than ten feet away!*

*It's an eerie feeling when you know something bad is going to happen, and there is nothing you can do about it. I only had about a second before he hit me, but a lot of things happened in that short amount of time.*

*My first thought, I think I spoke it out loud, was, "Oh, shit!"*

*At the same time, my foot flew to the brake pedal; I remembered a previous time when I had been hit in the rear, and violently pushed into the car in front of me. At that time I determined to put on the brakes if it ever happened again.*

*Then the Buick behind me began to crumple the rear of my beautiful, copper-colored Olds. I was thrown forward by* the impact. It felt like I was moving in slow motion, and then an angel's arms grabbed me and held me tight, keeping me from being hurt. It was probably the seat belt doing its job, but it sure felt like an angel's arms to me.

As I settled back into my seat, I recalled my involuntary remark, "Oh, shit!" and remembered a book I had just finished reading, <u>Millennium</u> by John Varley. In the book we were told when investigators listened to the little black boxes from commercial airplane crashes, eighty percent of the time the final words of the pilot are, "Oh, shit!" It was curious that my involuntary exclamation was the same.

As things began to settle down, I found myself observing what was going on around me. Putting on the brakes had been a smart decision. I had barely nicked the small pickup, pushing it ahead just a little.

As I sat there and watched, I saw a woman get out of the truck. She glanced around like she was in a fog, and then she started shouting at the sky. She wasn't looking at me; she didn't seem to be blaming me ... she was just shouting. Later on, when we met and exchanged insurance information, she was very nice. I don't think she even remembered the shouting.

As I was watching the woman's response to the accident, I was also looking in my rear-view mirror, wondering what the person who had hit me would do. Finally I saw the car door open, and out stepped a man who looked to be about eighty years old. He slowly walked up to my driver's side door. As he approached, I rolled down my window.

"Are you okay?" he asked.

"Yes, are you?"

"I think so," he said. After a long pause, he asked, "What do we do now?"

I figured it was about time to get out of my car; so I undid my seat belt, opened the door, and stepped out onto the freeway.

"Let's see how bad the damage is and then get these cars off to the side of the road," I said.

We walked around to the back of my car and saw that the entire right rear assembly was wrapped around the rear wheel. He had turned to the right just before hitting me, completely crumpling the right rear of my car, without even damaging the left. There was no way we were going to be able to push my car off the road.

I flagged down a van going down the off-ramp and asked the driver to please call the highway patrol. Almost immediately a voice blasted out from the heavens, "Get those cars off this freeway!" Right behind the Buick sat a California Highway Patrol car. Boy, was that fast service!

I walked around to the driver's side, and the officer rolled down his window.

"Is that your car up there?" he asked.

"Yes, sir," I said. "The small Olds up in front of the Buick."

"Well, get it off this freeway!" he demanded.

"It's not going anywhere without a tow-truck," I said.

He looked out his window and saw what looked like a car with only minor damage; he could only see the left side. He gave me a look that said, " You don't know what you're talking about."

"The right rear is wrapped around my right wheel," I explained.

He sighed, opened his door, got out of his car, and walked around to the right side of mine.

"Oh, shit!" he said. John Varley evidently knew what he was talking about.

A few minutes later, Jim (the man who had hit me) and I were standing out in the middle of the freeway waiting for the tow-truck to arrive, and the officer to begin taking down our statements.

Jim said, "Can I ask you a question?"

"Sure."

"Why did you stop?"

I thought, ... "Why did I stop? I stopped because all of the cars in front of me were stopped!" I looked in front of my car for all of those cars, so I could show Jim why I stopped ... the freeway was clear, not a car in sight. I looked behind us, and there all the cars were, somehow magically moved from in front of my car to behind the highway patrolman's car. Then I noticed the small pickup to the side of the road. (She'd moved over when she heard the voice from heaven.)

"See that pickup to the side of the road?"

"Yes."

"I stopped because that pickup was stopped," I replied.

"Oh," he paused. "Why did it stop?"

At this point I realized Jim was not aware of the facts concerning rush-hour traffic; he probably had never internalized that there was such a thing.

"You don't drive the freeways much at this time of the night, do you?" I asked.

"I never drive the freeways, and I never drive at night!"

"Then why did you drive out here tonight?"

"My wife and I got home from the store this afternoon about 3 p.m. When we entered the house, we found our son Joe having a heart attack. He told us to take him to the Veteran's Hospital in Palo Alto; we live in Cupertino. So we got him into the car, and I drove him there as fast as I could.

"I got him there in time, and got him checked into a room and everything; but by the time I got through, it was getting dark. I must have made a wrong turn someplace, because I got lost. Finally, I got out onto the freeway and saw a sign directing the traffic to Cupertino. I got on that road and was going along smoothly, when all of a sudden you were stopped dead in front of me. I couldn't stop in time."

I thought to myself, "This poor guy ... he gets home, finds his son having a heart attack, does the best he can for him, gets lost on the way home in the dark, and then has a traffic accident."

"I hope your son will be okay," I said. "How are you going to get home from here?"

"I don't know," he answered forlornly.

"Well ... if your car is drivable, and I'm sure it is, I could drive you home in your car," I offered.

"Would you really do that?"

"Sure, it's no problem."

At this moment, the highway patrolman reappeared and took down our statements. After he finished he looked at Jim and said, "Even though your car is drivable, I'm going to have it towed; I can't let you drive home."

"Jim and I have arranged for me to drive him home in his car, if that's okay with you, officer," I replied.

"Would you like him to do this for you?" he asked Jim.

"Yes, I would."

"Well, it's fine with me. I'll cancel the second tow-truck."

A few minutes later we were driving in Jim's car and he said to me, "You know, you don't have to take me all of the way home. My younger son John lives in Sunnyvale; you can take me there."

We drove over to John's house, and I walked up to the door. I knocked and John opened the door. As he looked out what he saw was a stranger standing on the porch, while his father was hanging back, standing on the walkway, seemingly afraid to face his son. The look John gave me was full of questions and suspicion.

"There was an accident on the freeway. Everyone is okay, but the highway patrol wouldn't let your dad drive his car home, so I offered to bring him here," I explained.

"Well, come in. You don't have to stand out there in the cold," he replied.

After we had been settled comfortably in the living room, John said, "Tell me what happened."

Jim began, "It started when your mom and I got home from the store and found Joe having a heart attack ... ."

It's funny the way people respond to pressure. After the shock of hearing about his brother's heart attack and the resulting accident, John was intent on discovering how his dad had gotten lost. Then he had to make his dad understand what he had done wrong and why he never should have made that wrong turn.

It became pretty embarrassing, so I finally said, "You know, John, I've been to that Veteran's Hospital in the daytime, and I've still had problems finding my way back to the right road to take me home. I'm not surprised your dad had trouble in the dark."

"Well ... you're probably right," he said. And we were finally able to get on to other things ... like finding someone to take me home.

## Chapter Nineteen     *This Isn't Funny*

My belief that I always know what is best for me was put to the test when I needed major surgery to correct bleeding ulcers at age forty-five. But I'm getting ahead of my story...

*I had suffered from a chronic cough for four months and was tired of putting up with it, so I went to see a doctor who specialized in such things. After a battery of tests, he concluded I had asthma and prescribed some medicine he thought would help. But he warned me it might make me feel a little weak.*

*I thanked him and left the office determined to follow his advice. I often have problems following the advice of doctors, and I have to make a conscious effort to do so.*

*Within twenty-four hours of that office visit and taking the new medication, I began to feel extremely weak. The weakness got so bad that I couldn't walk into our house from the car without having to lie down and rest for a few minutes.*

*It so happened my mother was staying with us at the time, because my father was in the hospital recovering from a heart operation (he had to have a new heart valve installed). During dinner we discussed who would be visiting Dad that night.*

*"I'm feeling kind of tired so I don't think I'm going to go," I said.*

*"I'm worried about your tiredness. Have you noticed any other symptoms?" my mother asked.*

*"You're always worried about my health, Mom. The doctor told me I could expect this to happen."*

*"Well, I am your mother ... have you noticed anything else?"*

"Yes, I have," I said and described the symptoms to her.

"You know, Brad, those symptoms are the same as the symptoms for a bleeding ulcer and massive blood loss. Maybe you should go and have it checked."

"But the last time I had an ulcer, I had lots of pain; this time, I'm experiencing no pain at all."

"Sometimes there is no pain; that's called a silent ulcer. What harm would there be in going to the clinic and having it checked?"

I agreed it couldn't hurt to have it checked. So I called the doctor and told him what was going on. He said it was only a drug reaction, but if I felt better having somebody check me, to go down to the urgent care facility.

After I hung up, we decided I would drive down to the clinic while Kathie and Mom would go visit Dad. Then we would meet back at the house afterwards.

At the clinic, the first thing they did was take my blood pressure. Then they asked me to lie down and took my blood pressure again. Then they asked me to stand up, and took my blood pressure a third time. Then they took a blood sample.

A short time later the doctor came into the examining room and took my blood pressure again, both laying down and standing up. Then he shook his head and walked out of the room.

The examining room was next to his office and, since he left my door open, I could hear him make a phone call.

"Dr. Johnson, this is Dr. Smith at the Urgent Care Facility. ... okay but, ... but Dr. Johnson, you are listed here as the doctor on call tonight. ... I'm sorry, sir, I won't bother you again."

I heard him dial again, and then he said, "Hello, Dr. Robbins, this is Dr. Smith at the Urgent Care Facility, and I wonder if you could help me out? ... I know, sir, but the doctor who I thought was on call says that he's not, and I really need to consult with someone about this case. ... I'm sorry, sir ... I won't bother you again."

*He hung up the phone, sighed deeply, and a few seconds later he was at my door.*

"Is there something I can do to help?" I asked.

*He looked surprised I would be asking him that question and then explained,* "It's just that your symptoms are confusing me."

"Well, maybe talking it over with me will help you understand what's going on," *I said.*

*He looked at me thoughtfully for a couple of seconds and then said,* "The results of your blood pressure readings lead us to believe you have had a massive loss of blood. But the results of the blood analysis seem to say that isn't true, and I don't know which to believe."

"What about the blood analysis makes you believe I haven't lost a lot of blood?" *I asked.*

"Your white blood cell count is normal. After losing a lot of blood, the white blood cell count is usually up significantly."

"Could it be I have lost the blood so quickly, and so recently, the white blood cell count has not had a chance to rise yet?" *I asked.*

"That could be it," *he mumbled softly to himself as he walked back to his office. It was time for me to give Kathie a call.*

*I got up from the examining table and walked down the hall, looking for a phone I could use.*

*The first nurse I saw asked,* "What do you think you're doing?"

"Looking for a phone," *I answered.*

"Well, you can't be walking around," *she said.* "Sit down in that chair. I'll get you a wheelchair." *Then she wheeled me to a phone.*

"Hello, Kathie, it's Brad ... things are getting interesting here. I think you'd better have Mom drive you over; there's not a chance they're going to let me drive anywhere."

*After the call, I was taken back to the examining room and told to get back up on the table. Then Dr. Smith came* in and said, "I think you should go over to the hospital now. How did you get here?"

"I drove," I answered.

"You can't drive to the hospital. Can somebody come and get you, or should we call an ambulance?"

"My wife is on her way over," I said. "I just called her."

"Good. Now when you get to the hospital, they're going to want to put a tube down your throat to find out what is going on down there."

"No way they're going to put a tube down my throat!" I responded.

"They need to, if they are going to be able to help you," he replied.

"Don't get me wrong," I said, "I'm not against it. It's just the last time I had a major illness, the doctors and nurses tried for hours to put a tube down my throat; and they never were able to get it down."

"We'll see ... in the meantime, I'll make arrangements for a doctor to meet you there." I heard him go back into his office and pick up the phone to make another call.

"Dr. Thomas? ... This is Dr. Smith at the Urgent Care Facility. I know you're not on call and I'm sorry to have bothered you, but I need some help here and I don't know who else to call." Then he paused, "You don't mind that I'm calling? Oh, thank you, sir."

Dr. Smith described my symptoms to Dr. Thomas and ended by saying, "His wife is coming to take him to the hospital. I will have him meet you at Emergency as quickly as possible. Thank you again!"

Right at that moment Kathie walked into the examining room. "Well, it looks like you're going to be taking me over to El Camino Emergency," I greeted her.

"Okay," she said. "What's going on?"

I explained what had transpired, and then Dr. Smith came in to tell us we were to meet Dr. Thomas at El Camino Hospital Emergency as soon as we could get over there. As he left the room he turned around to say, "Dr. Thomas wanted me to tell you he would have to put a tube down your throat, but not to worry; he is one of the best in the world at doing that procedure."

I smiled, thanked him for his hard work, and we were on our way.

As we drove to the hospital, I wondered how long we would be waiting once we arrived. I had been to emergency rooms in the past, and it always seemed like it took forever before it was my turn.

Kathie dropped me off at the door, and I waited while she parked the car. Then we walked into Emergency, and I told the nurse at the desk my name and mentioned we were expected.

"Mr. Fregger!" she exclaimed. And then turning her head she hollered, "Mr. Fregger is here!"

Suddenly a gurney appeared with a nurse and two aides holding intravenous setups containing saline solution. They pushed me onto the gurney, shoved the needles into my arms, started the saline solution, and then rolled me down the hall into an examining room. Kathie came along and I said to her, "That didn't take too long!"

A few minutes later a doctor came into the room. "I'm Dr. Thomas," he said. "How are you doing?"

"Fine," was my knee-jerk response.

"I have to find out what is going on in your stomach," he said. "But I've decided not to use a tube." Relief that I wouldn't have to go through that procedure flooded through me. "I've decided to use a television camera instead," he added smiling. "Don't worry, I am very good at this," and with that he left the room. My relief was short-lived!

A couple of minutes later two nurses came into the room, both holding hypodermic needles. The head nurse said her needle contained sodium-pentathol, while the other contained a Valium solution.

"The drugs will be administered with the saline solution," the head nurse said. "In a few short minutes you won't care what the doctor does to you."

As the drugs entered my system, I felt myself drifting off to never-never land.

The next thing I knew, I was sitting up in some sort of operating studio with something down my throat. Dr. Thomas asked how I was doing.

"Just fantastic," I slurred. I was filled with the high produced by the combination of the two drugs having been fed directly into my blood stream. "You can stick tubes down my throat anytime you want," I mumbled.

When I regained consciousness again, I was back in the examining room and Dr. Thomas was waiting there to talk with me. When he saw I was awake, and after checking to see that I was back to normal, he said, "You have a gusher down there. The ulcer is so bad that your blood is being pumped into your stomach; I could actually see it spout each time your heart beat. We'll have to operate immediately. I've already called a surgeon."

"Wait a minute ... I have no doubt you're right about the bleeding; but if there's going to be surgery, there's only one surgeon that operates on this body. You can tell the surgeon you've called he doesn't have to come down."

"Who's your surgeon?" he asked.

"Dr. Joseph Ignatius," I said. And Dr. Thomas paled. "What if he's out of town and we can't reach him?"

"First, let's see if he's available."

Five minutes later he was back. "Dr. Ignatius' exchange says he's unavailable. It's important we operate tonight. I should arrange for that right now."

"I don't think the emergency is that great. I'll make you a deal. You put me into intensive care and watch my signs—I know there are drugs that slow down bleeding.

"If the bleeding isn't stopped by tomorrow morning, I'll let you operate. If the bleeding does stop, we'll wait until Monday and try to locate Dr. Ignatius again. If he's still not available, I'll go with your surgeon. Okay?"

*He looked at me for a few moments, then said, "Okay," and left the room. Soon the nurses returned and took me to intensive care.*

---

*Kathie told me later when Dr. Thomas came back from trying to call Dr. Ignatius, he approached her and said, "Your husband is a very sick man ... he's lost three quarts of blood, and he won't let me operate. He says he wants Dr. Ignatius and I can't reach him."*

*Kathie couldn't believe she'd heard him right (having never heard of someone losing three quarts of blood), and her response was to laugh.*

*"This isn't funny," he said. "Your husband is bleeding to death."*

*She didn't know quite how to respond, so she said, "Brad usually knows what's best and he has strong opinions. I'd suggest you talk it over with him."*

*Dr. Thomas looked at her for a moment and finally said, "Okay."*

---

*The next day, Saturday, the intensive care day nurse came running into my room with a look of concern on her face. She stopped when she saw me and said, "I was looking for Mr. Fregger. The chart said he was back in this room."*

*"I'm Mr. Fregger. But this is my first time in this room. Maybe you mean my father, who's also in this hospital. Was he in this room recently?" I knew my dad had been in intensive care, but I didn't realize I was in the same room (actually the same bed) he had been in just one day before.*

*"So, Rolly's your father? You gave me a start. He's had such a tough time, and when I left I thought he'd finally made it. Then I saw your name on the chart and thought Rolly was back again."*

*I thanked her for her concern and asked what room my dad had been moved to. Then I picked up the phone.*

"Hi, Dad," I said.

"Hi, Brad. What are you doing?"

"I'm lying here in bed taking it easy."

"It's Saturday, isn't it? Aren't you going to do something special today?"

"Actually the bed I'm lying in is right downstairs. I was admitted to the hospital last night and I'm in intensive care right now—the same room and bed you just vacated."

"My God! What happened?"

"I was feeling kind of weak, and it turned out I have a bleeding ulcer and I've lost a lot of blood. It looks like I'm going to have my stomach operated on sometime in the next couple of days."

"How are you feeling right now?"

"I'm feeling fine. I don't think there's anything to worry about." *We talked a few more minutes and then hung up.*

---

*What happened next is, I think, why I ended up in the hospital at just that time. After my dad hung up the phone, he burst into uncontrollable sobbing and cried for a long time. He cried for his son and the operation he was soon going to have.*

*Dad had been having a very rough time and, in fact, came very close to dying. During the course of his recovery, his doctors told him if he thought he had it tough, he should be glad he wasn't having a stomach operation. "Stomach operations make heart operations look like a cakewalk," he told my dad. Now he'd learned that his son was in intensive care, waiting to have a stomach operation.*

*He couldn't handle the bad news, and the tears came flooding down. That was the best thing that could have happened. He couldn't cry for himself, but he needed the therapy that comes from a good cry. Now he could cry for his son, and he cried long and hard.*

*From that moment on, my dad began to get well, began to live again. I honestly believe without that cry, his healing process would have taken much longer; and he might never have completely healed. But he did heal fully, and has lived many, many more years as a healthy, vibrant individual.*

---

*On the following Monday I reached Dr. Ignatius, told him what was going on, and he was at my side within the hour. He operated on Tuesday.*

*My recovery went smoothly, and I never seemed to doubt it would. A week later I felt ready to be released. I also didn't like what they were feeding me in the hospital, so I told Dr. Ignatius I could do better feeding myself. I was released (they had removed half of my stomach), and I went home to be in charge of my own recovery from that point on.*

*One week later, I went to Dr. Ignatius to see how I was doing. After the examination, he proclaimed I was healing nicely and could eat anything I wanted, in any quantity that felt comfortable. "You know better than anyone how to take care of yourself," he added. Then he started to laugh.*

*"What's so funny?" I asked.*

*"I wish I could have seen the look on Dr. Thomas' face when you told him, 'Nobody touches my body but Dr. Ignatius,'" he said with a big grin.*

*Then he went on, "Everyone should take responsibility for their own health like you do. If they did, they'd have a much better chance of getting well."*

*I thanked him for the compliment. Then as he was leaving the room he turned to me and said, "I <u>am</u> the best there is when it comes to stomachs."*

*"I know," I said. "Why do you think I insisted on having you?"*

*He looked at me, smiled, and left the room.*

*I got dressed and went home to pick up Kathie. Then we went out together for lunch, a hamburger at Burger King. It was one of the most delicious hamburgers I have ever had.*

## Chapter Twenty  Stranger Than Fiction

Picking up where we left off in the previous chapter, the end of the second week found me feeling as good as new. However, Activision said I had to take a full six weeks off work. They felt having half your stomach removed demanded more than two weeks of recovery time. I had another four weeks to do whatever I wanted. What should I do? The perfect project soon occurred to me.

My son Jeff has had two highly unusual experiences in his life. The first happened when he was approximately ten and the second when he was an adult. One day it dawned on me these experiences would be a terrific basis for a science fiction film. During this convalescence from my stomach operation, I would write the preliminary script.

I had my script completed within a couple of weeks and decided it was good enough to show to a Hollywood producer. A friend and business associate, Ed Bogas,[19] agreed to take the script to Hollywood on his next trip and show it to some movie producer associates of his. Their judgment of the script turned out to be rather ironic ... but we'll get to that later.

### Electronic Dreams

*The movie opens in an immense warehouse containing thousands of white cylinders, each one designed and built to provide life support to a human being. It's difficult to tell*

---

[19] A Grammy nominated composer, Ed Bogas has scored hundreds of animated television shows, series and films featuring such illustrious characters as Fritz the Cat, Charlie Brown, Garfield and Betty Boop.

exactly what's going on, but it appears that people are getting into these cylinders ... and then being put to sleep.
The scene fades out. ...
The next scene opens in a young boy's bedroom. Ten-year-old Jeff is getting ready for school. He picks up his books and backpack and heads down the stairs.

His mother is in the kitchen and hears him coming, "We'll be leaving in about ten minutes, Jeff," she yells to him.

"Okay, Mom," he shouts back.

Jeff enters the living room and sets his books and backpack down in the middle of the floor. Lying down beside them, he stretches out full length. As he appears to be nodding off to sleep, his body jerks and. ...

All of a sudden there are two Jeff's, one slightly transparent—standing and looking down at the other Jeff still lying on the floor. The standing Jeff is confused. What in the world has happened? How can he be there on the floor and standing here looking at himself at the same time?

He turns his head toward the entryway to the kitchen and realizes he hears his mother preparing his school lunch box. He walks to the entryway and watches his mother working, then looks back at his body lying on the living room floor.

"I'm almost finished," his mother says. "Get your books and backpack, and I'll meet you at the car."

Jeff looks at his mother, then back at his body on the floor. What should he do? Finally, he walks over to his body and lays down on top of it ... actually he thought he was going to lay down on it ... instead, he lays down in it. He closes his eyes and opens them again ... he's back in his body and there's only one of him now. He stands up and goes out to the car to wait for his mother.

About 9 p.m. that night:

Jeff's in bed. His dad is sitting on the bed talking to him.

Jeff says, "Something funny happened today, Dad."

"Tell me about it."

"Well, ... I was waiting for Mom to take me to school, and I laid down on the floor. All of a sudden, ... " and he tells his dad the story. "What happened?" he asked.

"Let me ask you a couple of questions first, okay?"

"Okay."

"When you were in that other body, did everything seem crystal clear or kind of foggy?"

"It was crystal clear ... if anything even clearer than I see things right now."

"You said, 'All of a sudden I was standing up, looking down at my body.' Did you hear or feel a kind of 'pop' just before you found yourself standing there?"

"I felt kind of a pop ... I don't know if I heard anything."

"I think I know what happened. While it's a pretty unusual experience, you're not the only one to have had it. It's called soul travel or astral projection."

"What's that mean?"

"Well, you know how you put your clothes on before you go to school?" Jeff nods his head. "And you know how you learn at church that people have souls ... the something that is the real us that continues to live after we die?"

"Yes," Jeff replies, listening intently.

"Can you see how your body might be something your soul wears, so it can live in the world?"

"Okay ... I guess so."

"Well ... some people believe it's possible to leave our material body and walk around, or travel, in our soul body. That's why they call it soul travel, or a more fancy term is astral projection. I think you had an experience of soul travel ... for a short time, you left your material body and walked around in your soul body. That's pretty special!"

"Then, it's okay, ... I'm not sick or crazy or anything?"

"No ... you're not crazy. You simply had a very unusual experience most people never get to have, at least in this life.

*I would be interested in knowing if it ever happens again. Good night, son ... see you tomorrow."*

*Twenty years later ... the interior of an electronics plant:*

*Jeff is busy at a workbench when Tom, one of his fellow workers, enters the area and says, "Jeff, we're needed at Fab 3 right away!"*

*"What's up?" Jeff asks as he gets up and follows Tom out the door.*

*"One of the implanters is arcing, and we need to take a look at it."*

*Jeff and Tom enter Fab 3, walk up to the implanter, and turn it on. It is obviously arcing. As Jeff opens the service door, the implanter turns off.*

*"Tom, hold the auto-shutoff while I take a look inside."*

*"Okay, but be careful!"*

*Jeff, trying to get a better look, sticks his head into the body of the implanter. He sees the arcing as a flash of brilliant white light fills his field of vision.*

*When he can see again, he's standing on the crest of a hill. Down at the bottom of the hill is an Old World style inn. It's dark but he can see a light glowing inside. There are no stars. He's confused ... concerned, "I must have been dreaming about work ... and now I've shifted to another dream ... what else could it be?" he thinks.*

*He decides to walk down to the inn. When he gets there, he goes up to the front door and opens it.*

*He looks into a sparsely furnished room cloaked in darkness. On the other side of the room stands a being, not human, difficult to see, almost as if it were draped in shadows. The being is holding light—it has no shape or substance—only light, pure and simple.*

*"That's mine," Jeff thinks, as he is flooded with the knowledge that the light belongs to him. Then he thinks, "How am I going to get it? ... whatever is holding it may not give it to me willingly."*

*Jeff walks over to the being and quickly plunges his hand and arm into the light.*

*Then. ...*

*He finds himself standing next to the implanter, looking at the service door, which is still standing open. He feels a little sick and very worried.*

*"I feel funny ... I think I'm catching the flu," Jeff says out loud, to no one in particular.*

*"What do you mean?" Tom says alarmingly. "You just took 25,000 volts of electricity! God, are you alright?"*

*Jeff realizes only a second or two has passed since the flash of white light filled his vision. Yet, it seemed that he spent at least fifteen minutes in that other world.*

*He looks at Tom and says, "I think so, but my leg hurts."*

*His pant leg is burned. They pull the burned fabric aside and find a starburst pattern of broken blood vessels on his leg.*

*"That's strange ... I wonder what happened?" Jeff thinks.*

*Later that night Jeff calls his dad and relates his experience. "What do you think happened?" Jeff asks.*

*"The incident you describe is similar to experiences described by those who hover near death. How did it feel? Was it like a dream, or like real life?"*

*"It felt as real as any dream I've ever had. I was aware of everything going on around me; the tall grass on the hillside, the darkness, yet lack of stars. But ... it was more like a vivid dream than real life. It didn't feel as real as the time when I found myself standing outside of my body. Remember? ... "*

*"Oh yes ... I remember."*

At this point the film truly does becomes fiction. We discover a deranged computer is holding humanity hostage and that the world we think is true is only a creation of the computer's mind. It becomes Jeff's responsibility to "defeat" the computer and save humanity.

Both of the experiences I described actually happened to my son Jeff, including the conversations with Dad.

When Ed got back from Hollywood, here's what he told me, "They found the script interesting but thought it definitely needed more work. They were bothered only by the part where the protagonist has those weird experiences and his conversations with his dad ... they said nobody would ever believe that!"

**Sometimes truth is stranger than fiction.**

I got a call from Jeff right after he saw *The Matrix*, "Hey, Dad ... just saw your movie. It was great!"

# Part Five

## *Life-Changing Stories*

## Chapter Twenty-One    *Creating the Story*

Stories often have multiple goals. Some are obvious. Some are hidden. Some are unknown even to the teller.

Sometimes stories are told for pure entertainment. Sometimes their purpose is to entertain and subtly teach, inspire, or foster change. And sometimes the story's purpose is to entertain and teach, inspire or cause change without the listener even knowing it.

We may also want to create a story for a specific situation. The situation might involve a group of people, a family, a team, a company or an organization. However, in my experience, it most often involves a single individual who is struggling with an issue that may not be solvable unless there is a change in the way the person perceives the situation.

Stories to change beliefs, attitudes, and perceptions are used to empower others; these stories have a direct and positive impact on the person's capability to live his or her life successfully. The objectives of this type of storytelling are to:

1) *Help individuals make the changes needed for personal and career success,*
2) *Inspire individuals to achieve beyond their normal capabilities,*
3) *Help individuals deal with change, and*
4) *Help individuals handle hard times.*

To accomplish any of these four objectives, a story must have two essential characteristics. The first characteristic is:

**The story contains a description of the problem or situation without relating directly to it (using metaphor or "personal story").**

The characters in the story must be struggling with an issue that mirrors the situation confronting the individual.

This is handled in several different ways in the stories following this chapter. For example, in the first story, *Good News*, the person is not handling retirement well, believing his life is over. The story told to him relates to a younger man who has just sold his business. The situations are a reflection of each other, but they are not identical.

A very different approach was used with *The Story of Fred*. In this instance, the individual was having problems dealing with the infidelity of her husband and didn't know how she could ever trust him again. The story given her was a fable that reflected infidelity without mentioning it. In addition, the issue of trusting that the problem would not recur was also reflected in the fable.

The second essential characteristic is:

☞ **The story provides the unconscious mind with the solution for the problem the individual is confronting, including specific changes needed to bring about the desired result.**

The story must have all of the ingredients of the current situation and then provide an alternative that will bring about the best possible outcome. Usually this will mean that the individual must change the way they are thinking about and/or responding (or reacting) presently.

The story shows how what they are currently doing is NOT working, and how a change in attitude could result in the ideal solution.

Here are some final guidelines for creating stories that change beliefs, attitudes, and perceptions.

**1) Don't explain the message in the story.**

This is the most critical guideline of all. It is also the most difficult for the storyteller to deal with. Many people have a compelling need to explain what they are doing and why they are doing it. Whenever you involve the conscious mind, the potential effectiveness of the story is greatly diminished; in fact, the story may lose its effectiveness entirely. If you doubt this, go back and reread chapter one, *How the Mind Works*, and chapter two, *How Stories Work*.

This rule must be kept in mind during the entire planning process. Remember to tell the story in such a way that it is not obvious what you are doing.

**2) When the reason is obvious, storyteller credibility determines effectiveness.**

If it is obvious why you are telling the story, then it is critical that you have excellent credibility with the person you're telling the story to. For example, a respected superior in the workplace could probably get away with it; a dad telling the story to his daughter may not. You need to look at this very honestly ... sometimes we believe we have more credibility than we actually do.

**3) Plan carefully making sure to have the goal and ways of attaining it well in mind.**

It is critical to have the desired outcome clearly in mind. There can be no doubt as to what you are trying to accomplish. We don't experiment with this process ... we don't try something out just to see what will happen.

**4) It's important to keep things as simple and direct as possible.**

- *What's the basic issue?*
- *What changes would make the difference?*
- *Does the story contain a description of the problem without relating directly to it?*
- *Does it also contain information providing the unconscious with a potential solution for the problem?*

**5) Use "real stories" whenever possible; but remember, metaphor can also do the job.**

The story itself is usually delivered as a "personal story" or metaphor. A "personal story" is one represented as a true experience of the storyteller or a personal acquaintance. Metaphors are usually not "true," but rather legends or fables presented as allegory, which are representative of the problem or situation and the solution.

"Real stories" can be especially powerful, because it is easier to hide the purpose for telling the story. And we have seen this is critical. When telling people about something that happened to you personally, they usually don't wonder why they're being told; they listen, commiserate, and move on.

For most of us, it seems to work better if the story we're telling is from our own personal experience. While it is permissible to create a story and then tell it as if it really happened to us, I have discovered it's easier and more credible if you can find one that really happened, either to you personally or to someone you know.

Finally, if you do decide to use metaphor or create a "fable," it's often better to put it in writing and give it to the person to read. For most of us, this type of story seems to be more effective when read. There may be exceptions... you'll have to go with your own feeling about it.

6) Treat "change effecting" stories as silver bullets; don't overdo them.

While it may seem awkward in the beginning, if you persevere, you will soon discover good things happen when you use stories in this way. With this reinforcement, you will be tempted to use stories more and more often ... resist this temptation! Life-changing stories should be used sparingly, only when the situation is critical.

I'll never forget the day I learned this lesson.

## It Was a Hoot!

*As Vice President of Product Development for a software company in Austin, Texas, I had responsibility for much of the development. However, the company had signed a contract with Microsoft for a new game, and the President wanted to be the senior manager for this "critical project."*

*About a quarter of the way through the project, the Art Director quit. This was a disaster and, to make matters worse, the president was out of town. The Project Manager came to me in a panic and said, "What are we going to do? While this is bad enough, what if some of our artists go with him?"*

*"Would you like me talk to everyone, see where we stand and try to assure the rest of the team will stay?" I asked.*

*"That would be great," she said, the relief obvious in her voice.*

*I spent most of that day talking to everyone in the company, finding out how they felt about the Art Director's departure, while making sure we had their commitment to stay with us through the end of the project.*

*My usual approach in tough times is to share stories from my past that relate to the specific needs of each individual; this time was no exception.*

When I was through, the Project Manager and I got together and shared how the day had gone. We were both confident everyone else would be staying. With the crisis over, she began to laugh.

"What's so funny?" I asked.

"You provided us with something to talk about all day long," she replied.

"What do you mean?"

"Well, whenever anyone came out of your office, we'd all pounce on them and demand to know which story you told. We kept a tally ... it was a hoot!"

---

It appears I had overdone it! My future ability to use stories to change attitudes within that group had been seriously compromised. But I learned an important lesson ... and had a good laugh at myself.

## Chapter Twenty-Two  *Good News*

A couple of years ago I decided to call a close friend of mine I hadn't talked to for a while. I heard her husband had finally retired, and I wondered how things were going.

Shortly after we'd said our hellos, I sensed she was very concerned about something. A few minutes into the conversation she started crying, which was very unusual. Then she said, "I'm so worried about Bob. He's not handling his retirement well at all. We had a trip planned to Europe; but now he says he's not interested in going, not interested in doing anything, except maybe calling it quits. I've talked, and talked but nothing seems to help."

"What did he mean by 'calling it quits'?" I asked.

"He acts like he isn't interested in going on living ... that's what I'm so worried about. I can do without the Europe trip ... but I don't want to lose Bob."

"I'm sorry to hear he's feeling that way. Is there anything we can do?"

"You've done a lot just by listening. Maybe you could say a prayer or two to help us through this time."

The conversation continued on a lighter vein for a few more minutes and then I said, "By the way, I just finished reading a great book I'd love to share with you. Barbara and I have to drive by your house at about four this afternoon. Would it be convenient to drop it by then?"

"We'd love to see you ... four o'clock would be just fine," and we said our goodbyes.

After hanging up the phone, I went to Barbara and said, "Cheryl's really upset over Bob's reaction to his retirement. Not only doesn't he want to go to Europe, but he doesn't seem to be interested in anything and is even talking about dying. I'd like to go and see them this afternoon ... I told Cheryl I had a book I wanted to share with her ... we set four o'clock as a good time to stop by. Does this work for you?"

"Sure it does," she responded. "Some men have a rough time with retirement. Is there some way we could help?"

"Cheryl didn't think so ... What I thought I'd do is come up with a story to tell Bob while we're over there ... something that sounds natural but speaks to life after retirement. If I do this ... you'll go along with it, won't you?"

"Of course ... got something in mind?"

"Not right now, but I will by the time we get there."

During the trip to their home, I came up with a personal story I thought would do the trick.

About half way through the visit, when I noticed a little lull in the conversation, I said, "I got some good news today."

Bob replied, "What kind of news?"

"Did I tell you about my friend Jim and that it looked like he was going to be selling his business for a very nice profit?"

"I don't remember you telling me that."

"Well, about six months ago Jim had a chance to sell his business. The offer was too good to pass up, so he made the leap. The problem was, he thought he was going to be kept on as the manager. It turned out all they wanted was his technology and client list. He was left with no authority and no real job he could get his teeth into. He was getting real depressed."

"Big companies are like that ... they buy a successful company and then don't pay any attention to the things that made it successful. What did he do?" Bob seemed interested and unsuspecting of my motives.

"He called me this morning all excited. He's finally made up his mind to make a clean break with the past, forget about his old company, and take this opportunity to do a lot of the things he's always wanted to do but never had the time. He and his wife are leaving for Rio tomorrow! It was so good to hear his voice full of passion and excitement again."

Bob nodded and the conversation went off into other directions. We left a short time later.

*It was a week to the day when I got a call from Cheryl. I could hear the excitement in her voice as she said, "Brad, I just wanted you to know I haven't had a chance to get to that book yet. Bob and I are so busy getting ready for our trip to Europe ... did I tell you we decided to go after all?"*

---

Did the story make a difference? This question is unanswerable. There's no way to know what impact the story had on Bob's attitude toward retirement and the pending trip to Europe. I can't ask him if the story helped; I can't even ask Cheryl. There's an excellent chance they don't even remember I told them the story. The important thing is that for whatever reason, Bob's attitude shifted and he was interested in living once again.

## Chapter Twenty-Three  *The Story of Fred*

Tom and Sally were close friends and a happy couple. There was no doubt in my mind they were made for each other. Everything was going great; they had jobs they liked and two terrific kids. And then, a woman named Wendy joined the accounting firm where Tom worked.

Wendy was an attractive, intelligent woman with some personal problems, and Tom was a convenient shoulder to cry on. It's often dangerous when a sensitive, caring, but married man (or woman) gets too involved in the personal life of an attractive, intelligent person of the opposite sex. And sure enough, Tom quickly found himself in much deeper than he had intended.

The affair lasted a month or so before Sally found out ... she was devastated. Without a moment's hesitation she tossed Tom out of the house, along with most of his belongings. Tom quickly realized how stupid he'd been, broke off the affair, and tried to talk Sally into taking him back. But Sally was adamant; she couldn't live with a man she couldn't trust.

Tom spent a lot of time talking to me, berating himself for his stupidity, and asking me to intercede for him. I tried talking to Sally; but she saw me as a friend of Tom's, someone on his side, someone who could never understand the depth of her pain.

I couldn't stand back and do nothing ... I loved these people too much. So I sent Sally a story.

### *The Story of Fred*

*This is the story of Frederick Thompson Bartholomew Adair, Fred for short.*

*Fred lived in a small cottage in a small town somewhere around here. He loved his cottage, and he loved the land that surrounded it. It was a very ordinary cottage, and no matter how hard Fred worked, the land never produced a garden Fred could be proud of.*

*Fred purchased many books on gardening and gardens. He knew what he needed to do, but it just didn't work out the way it did in the books. At night, after a hard day weeding and watering, Fred would sit down in front of the fire and read about beautiful gardens from all over the world. These books contained the most wonderful pictures: pictures of small and large gardens, gardens with fountains and gardens without them, private gardens and gardens that were grown so passersby could enjoy them. As he read the books and looked at the pictures, he would dream of a time when he, too, would have a garden beautiful enough to be included in a book.*

*One night, while Fred was dreaming about his garden, a strange man came dancing down the road. If you had seen him, he surely would have turned your head. He stood about five feet tall, with slick, black hair that shown like obsidian in the moonlight. His ears were slightly pointed, and his eyes glowed and sparkled with what appeared to be the light of fireflies. He wore a jacket of soft green carpet moss, trousers from the lily pad, and shoes fashioned from redwood bark. His name was Pete, and he was a garden elf.*

*As Pete danced by Fred's house, he saw a garden lacking the spirit to support more than just the smallest amount of growth. He was struck by how pathetic the garden looked. It had obviously had a lot of work. The tools were* neatly placed in the shed, and bags of fertilizer could be seen stacked outside.

Pete had been looking for a garden for the longest time, but he didn't want just any old garden. He wanted a garden that would be loved and cared for, one that would be appreciated, and—most important—one that needed him. As he gazed around, he realized this was a garden that really needed him.

He walked into the garden and heard it call for his help, call for him to become a part of it. But Pete wasn't sure yet, so he went into the house to see Fred. He wanted to get to know the garden's owner before he made his final decision.

Fred was asleep when Pete entered, and Pete didn't wake him. He didn't need to because Pete could see into Fred's soul, could see into his dreams and his fears. What he found was a man who truly loved and appreciated beautiful things, gardens in particular. This was a man who would appreciate Pete's work and the beautiful garden that would result. Pete was convinced, and at that moment he dedicated himself to Fred's garden for all time.

The next morning when Fred woke and went out into his garden, he noticed the change immediately. He wasn't sure what had happened, but he saw some small wild flowers beginning to grow, and the air was rich with the smell of oxygen and the power of growing things. From that day on, whatever he planted took root immediately and grew with a beauty and ease beyond what Fred had believed possible. At the yearly fair he invariably won one or two gold ribbons, sometimes for his flowers, often for his fruit and vegetables. As the years passed, the garden became known throughout the land as a place of beauty, harmony and fertility.

Pete was true to his pledge for all of these many years and never once thought of moving on. Garden elves often went from garden to garden. But Pete was one of the elves that committed to a garden, and he liked the thought of staying with just one garden for all of his life.

*However, he had one weakness, some would say a flaw in his character. It was the thing that had drawn him to Fred's garden in the first place. He needed a garden that needed him; and as the years passed by, while he still loved Fred's garden deeply, he began to forget how much it needed him. It seemed so healthy, so capable of handling anything the weather or fates could throw at it.*

*One day Pete noticed a garden down the lane. This garden was in such ill repair. It looked like it had once been pretty, but now it was defeated, abandoned, and alone with its weeds and barren ground. He was drawn to it, and without thinking, he left Fred's garden and entered the one down the lane.*

*Fred noticed the difference almost immediately; the air didn't smell as good, and when he planted new plants, they had trouble taking hold and often died. He didn't know what to do—no matter how hard he worked—it just wasn't the same. For the first year, since Pete had come to his garden, he won no prizes at the fair.*

*Things went from bad to worse, until one day, without any warning, the blight came. When Fred got up that morning, all of the leaves in his garden were curled and dying, and a gray fungus had spread throughout. The air smelled of decay and death. Fred had to set a torch to all of the plants in his garden—it was the only way the blight could be stopped. He fired them all, as tears ran down his face and soiled his cheeks.*

*Pete noticed the smoke and wondered what was burning. Then he saw it was Fred's garden, and he knew immediately what had happened. "What have I done?" he thought. "Here I am struggling in a new garden, one that I haven't even committed to, while the garden I swore to remain with has been decimated." Guilt and sorrow spread through him like the fire he was forced to watch from afar, spreading through his beloved garden.*

*"I will return to the garden I swore to protect," he thought. "I can make it bloom again!"*

And so he returned with new commitment and determination, with a vow he would never again leave.

The next morning, as Fred looked out on his garden, he felt a dread he had never felt before. He knew what it was like to have a beautiful garden where everything would grow, and now he knew what it was like to lose that garden. The pain was more than he thought he could bear. As he walked into his barren garden, he sensed the smell of new fertility and somehow glimpsed the promise of new growth. But then the pain came flooding back, so Fred turned his back on the garden, tears flowing down his cheeks.

Pete watched all of this with a sad heart, but he was determined to bring back the beauty that had been there before. He worked tirelessly to make the garden fertile again, even capturing seeds from the wind. While Fred sometimes worked hard at planting new things, most of the new growth had to come from Pete. In time, with Pete's devoted efforts, the garden did become beautiful again. It didn't look quite like it had before; it wasn't as well ordered and abundant.

Fred didn't spend as much time in his garden either; somehow it hurt him to be near it for too long. But it had a beauty all its own, and people again began to mention how pleasant it was, and how much they wished they could have a garden as beautiful.

Pete kept hoping and praying Fred's pain would heal, and he would again be able to appreciate the love Pete was pouring into the garden. Hopefully he would sense the vow Pete had made—and know Pete would never leave the garden again.

But a strange thing happened. As Pete worked harder and harder on the garden, Fred's dreams became more and more depressing. In his dreams he would look out on his new garden, appreciating it; and then the blight would begin again, spreading through his garden as he watched. He would wake up screaming, with a pain that went deep into his soul. Soon Fred couldn't even see the garden Pete was creating; all he could see was the blight and the pain it had caused.

*One morning he couldn't take it anymore, and Fred decided he would tear out his garden and build a patio with a big swimming pool. He spent all day arranging for this and planned to begin work the next morning. Pete knew this was happening, but he didn't know what to do. If the patio and pool were put in, he would have to leave; he could only live in gardens—he was a garden elf. He'd made a vow to stay forever; but he couldn't live in this new environment and would die if he tried to stay.*

*All seemed lost, but that last night a miracle happened. In Fred's dream, just as the blight was about to cover the garden, Pete appeared and Fred saw him. All of a sudden, Fred realized Pete had been there all along, making the garden a beautiful place, and it was only in his dreams that the blight struck again. Now he could rest assured Pete would keep the blight away for as long as he lived.*

*As this realization happened, Pete smiled and the garden in Fred's dream bloomed to a perfection he had never dreamed of.*

*Fred woke the next morning knowing all would be well. He would have a beautiful garden again, in fact, already did have a beautiful garden! The first thing he did was cancel the construction of the patio and pool. Then he went out into his garden—seeing it as if for the first time, secure in the belief the blight would never return.*

---

Within a couple of weeks of my sending Sally *The Story of Fred*, she started a dialogue with Tom. That was over ten years ago, and Tom and Sally are still going strong!

*Chapter Twenty-Four*  **The Miracle Man**

*O*nce in a while something happens to reinforce your faith in the power of stories to change people in significant ways.

One day during the summer of *1995*, and I was sitting in my car at the intersection of Bernardo Avenue and El Camino Real in Sunnyvale, California, waiting for the light to change I noticed a young mother with a child in a stroller standing on the sidewalk next to me, also waiting. I watched as the "Walk" signal came on; then she entered the crosswalk, pushing the stroller ahead of her.

Next I noticed a car making a left turn directly into her path ... what was going on? Didn't he see her? I hit the horn at the same instant the car screeched to a halt ... just in time! Why had he gone? She had the "Walk" signal. Then I noticed my left-turn signal was green ... I couldn't believe it; <u>the left-turn signal and the "Walk" signal were on at the same time!</u> I was appalled.

As soon as I returned home, I was able to determine that the State of California was responsible for the light at that intersection. I immediately called them about the problem, only to be told the light was working as designed; and they had no intention of changing it. I was incensed and ended the conversation by saying, "A terrible accident is going to happen at that intersection; and when it does, it's going to be your fault!"

During the first week of January in *1999*, my dad and my former wife Kathie were standing at that same corner waiting for the light to change. When it did, they stepped into the crosswalk and started to cross the street. Then they noticed a car making a left turn and coming right at them

... they stopped and backed up ... the car stopped ... my dad went ... the car went. The terrible accident I predicted happened. I had no idea it would be my own father who would suffer.

My dad was very seriously injured, numerous bones broken in his pelvis and leg. He was in a drug-induced coma for ten days, only to awaken to massive pain. His chances for recovery, at eighty-three years old, weren't very good. He spent about a month in the Stanford Hospital and then was flown to a hospital in Billings, Montana, the city where Mom and Dad live most of the year.

While we were all very concerned about his body's ability to heal from such a major injury, we were just as concerned about his attitude. When I called him in the hospital, I was always saddened to hear his voice. He was difficult to understand, and all of his usual zest for life was missing. We were afraid the chances of his getting well, if he didn't have the will to, were not very good.

I was Chief Product Officer for a startup in Austin, Texas, at the time. One day in late February we were in a company planning session with an important advisor. The first thing he did was check with each of us to see if we were going to be ready to go to market by September. Marketing would be ready. Sales would be ready.

Then he looked at me and said, "How about Product Development? Are you going to be ready with the product?"

There was a moment of silence and then I replied, "There's no way we're going to be ready. We don't have a design specification for a product, only a visionary concept. In addition, we haven't even begun to hire our technical staff; you can't do a realistic technical design or schedule without input from the people who will be responsible for delivering the product."

This didn't go over well. In fact, the advisor looked up at us and said, "Let me know when this group's got its act together." Then he left the room.

With fire in his eyes, the Sales VP said, "I've been working seven months to help build a successful business, and you destroyed everything in a couple of minutes!"

Everyone else just looked sad. It was one of the worst days of my working life.

When I got home I told Barbara, "It isn't worth it. I'm fifty-eight and I've already been there and done it. I don't want to put up with this anymore. I think I'm going to give my notice." Then I told her what had happened.

Barbara was supportive and encouraging, but I still needed to vent. I called my son, "Jon, I need to talk ... have you got the time to listen?"

"Sure, Dad. What's the problem?" I told him my story. After I was through, he said, "Doesn't sound like my dad."

"What do you mean?"

"You know, Dad, being a minister isn't all peaches and cream. There are times when I just want to chuck the whole thing, quit worrying about all the politics, tell some of the people to go take a hike. You know what I say to myself when I feel that way?"

It seemed to be a rhetorical question, so I waited for him to answer it.

"I say, 'What would Dad do? Dad would look at me and say, 'When the going gets tough, Freggers get tougher!'"

I hate it when my kids throw my own words back at me like that! When we finished the conversation, I looked over at Barbara and said, "Jon talked me out of resigning ... they can fire me, but I won't quit. And I'll keep doing and saying what I know is right."

I took a deep breath, was silent for a moment, and then it hit me ... <u>this was the exact story I needed to tell Dad!</u>

He was having a tough time. The solution: "When the going gets tough, Freggers get tougher!"

Better yet, it was a real story, one I could easily share with honesty and passion.

*I called him immediately. He answered with the same hard to understand, lackluster voice that saddened me so. But as usual, he wanted to know, "How's your day been?"*

*"Probably the worst day of my working life," I said.*

*"What happened?" he asked with fatherly concern.*

*So I told him. At the end I said, "So you know what happened when I got home?"*

*"What?"*

*"I called Jon and told him my story. Do you know what he said? He said, 'You know what I say to myself when I feel that way? I say, What would Dad do? Dad would look at me and say, 'When the going gets tough, Freggers get tougher!"*

*There was a moment of silence, and then my dad asked, "What are you going to do?"*

*"I'm going to stick it out. They can fire me, but I'll be damned if I'm going to resign. And I'm not going to stop telling them what I think they need to hear either."*

*At that point the conversation turned to other things.*

*A few days later I called him and got the surprise of my life ... it was my old dad back again, his voice full of humor and that zest for life I had grown to love, "I can't talk for long, Brad. They're going to be here in a minute to take me to therapy, and I've got to get ready. It looks like I'll be going home in a couple of days, and there's no way I'm letting your mother take me to the bathroom."*

---

During the entire time of my Dad's illness, my brother Dennis had taken responsibility for keeping family and friends up-to-date on his progress. He did this with email messages; here's the final message that he sent to all those people who cared so very much.

## Dennis' Message

We arrived in Billings, Montana, on April 19th, my mother's 80th birthday. It was about 6 p.m. when I drove into my folk's garage. Mom opened the door from the kitchen immediately and greeted us with a big smile. As I stood at the kitchen door and looked through the kitchen into the living room, I was amazed to see my father walking towards me. His big smile belied his recent past, as did his limpless gait. He carried a cane, just in case, but didn't need it!

HE LOOKED EXACTLY AS HE HAD BEFORE THAT EARLY JANUARY DAY! We reveled in the wonder of it. I've begun to call him the "Miracle Man." He's not up to his regular two to four miles a day yet, but he's walking about a half to one mile presently. The transformation from when we last saw him is simply mind-boggling!

I'm convinced much of his improvement can be placed squarely on all of you beautiful people. Yeah, I know genetics was a great help, too; but all your cards, notes and e-mails simply blew Dad away! More than once he said, " I didn't know so many people cared!"

Thank you so much everyone! I'm so happy this last installment of my father's saga was full of joy.

I will always wish the same for you.

Love, Dennis

## Chapter Twenty-Five  *Auntie Perry*

*I* asked my wife Barbara to try her hand at writing a life-changing story. Here's what she wrote—just for you.

When I was a young girl, perhaps about nine, my mom's older sister, Jennie Perry, would often come for afternoon visits. Auntie Perry, as we called her, lived in a neighboring town some fifteen miles from our Iowa farm home. Often her husband, Uncle Burt (a story in himself), would come along, but sometimes Auntie came alone. Funny ... she was the only aunt (and we had many, since both my parents were from fairly large families) we called "auntie"... everyone else was "aunt" so and so, but she was Auntie Perry.

At this time, Auntie was about fifty-three (coincidentally my age now). She had two grown sons, who were older than my oldest siblings, and we younger children were not aware they even existed.

One day Auntie had just gone home after one of these visits, when my sister Janice, three years older than I, turned to Mom with a puzzled look on her face and asked, "Mom, how come Auntie Perry doesn't have any kids ... and we're all piled up with 'em[20]?" I'll never forget my mom's laughter. When she finally regained her composure, she patiently explained to us that Auntie Perry did indeed have two grown sons. We were amazed.

But Auntie Perry never had any little girls, and she evidently wanted a little girl to lavish attention on. Whenever she came, we would all get hugs and kisses, and I would squirm and feel embarrassed and awkward. We weren't a

---

[20] Barbara is the tenth of twelve children.

demonstrative family—there was lots of love, but not much hugging and kissing in our house. And this hugging and kissing stuff was hard to handle graciously when you weren't used to it. My squirming didn't stop Auntie—she continued to display her affection each time she came to visit.

Auntie called me Bobbie (while everyone else called me Barbie); and visit after visit, she would beg me to pack my suitcase and come home with her for a week or two. This would frighten me terribly, and I would run and hide. Safe in my hiding place, I would try to entertain the idea, but I was painfully shy. My worst fear was that she would be kissing and hugging me every day—how would I survive that?

But maybe there would be some other girls my age in her neighborhood? It might be fun ... she lived in town, after all ... and we lived in the country. I loved to go to town whenever Mom would let me. And Auntie was a great cook ... She was always bringing us pies, and cookies ... maybe she would even make my favorite—divinity with pecans on top!

But then Uncle Burt might tease me a lot ... and the thought of leaving the safety of my secure little world ... Mom ... Daddy ... the comfort of familiar surroundings—well, it was just too scary. No, I would hide upstairs until Auntie left, when it would be safe to venture back downstairs. And that's what I did, time after time.

I remember Auntie telling me, as a selling point, how Pat, my older sister by ten years, had come to stay with her when she was a little girl. She would tell me what fun they had cooking and sewing and gardening together (Auntie was an avid flower gardener) ... and didn't I want to come and have fun, too? But I would just stare at the floor and squirm ... and disappear first chance I got. Eventually Auntie quit asking, and I didn't have to run for cover any more. What a relief!

It wasn't until years later, as a college student living in the same town where Auntie lived, when it began to dawn on me that I had missed out. I don't remember what woke me up, but suddenly one day, quite out of the blue, the thought occurred to me to call Auntie Perry and ask if Kerry, my fiancé at the time, and I could come visit her and Uncle Burt. She was delighted, of course. It was the first time ever I had gone to visit her on my own ... and I hadn't even been coerced!

We had a great visit, and she sent me home with a beautiful bouquet of lilacs from her yard. As I enjoyed the heavenly fragrance of the lilacs the next few days, I thought about Auntie Perry and all those times she had begged me to come stay with her. What a silly little goose I had been to run and hide!

Why hadn't Mom insisted I go? Well, I knew the answer to that one! I was a very stubborn child, and Mom probably figured it was best to leave the decision to me. Now I realized, due to my stubbornness and timidity, I had missed out on some wonderful experiences. What's worse ... I had deprived Auntie and Uncle Burt of the joy of having a little girl to lavish their attention on, if only for awhile. Furthermore, I was sure it would have been good for me to have gotten some extra attention. If I could only go back and do it differently ... but, of course, it wasn't possible.

Happily, Auntie and I did become good friends during those several years when I lived nearby. And I was able to tell her how much I regretted not accepting those invitations as a little girl. But then I moved away, and our visits were less frequent.

A couple of years later, I moved way down to Texas and rarely got to see her at all, but we did talk on the phone from time to time. All too soon, in May of *1990*, I got the sad call saying Auntie had left us.

In the days following, I felt her spirit close around me; all I could think about was how much Auntie loved flowers. I remembered her back yard as it appeared on childhood visits (with the family along, of course!) and the pansies neatly planted along the walk and behind the house. She must have loved pansies ... they were everywhere. I'm sure her yard was loaded with all kinds of flowers, but for some reason, what I remember are the pansies. Later when they sold their home and moved into an apartment, she planted beautiful flowerbeds there ... lilies, roses, phlox, impatiens, and, I'm sure, pansies. Auntie's yard was colorful and inviting, and her fellow tenants were appreciative of her efforts. It was her therapy and her joy to be out in the yard digging.

I wasn't able to go home for her funeral. But on one of those sad days following her passing, I was sitting at my desk at work when a poem came to me. I quickly scribbled it down. It felt like Auntie's poem.

## *Wildflowers*
### by Barbara Foley

*My favorite flowers grow wild.*

*They shoot up from the ground
in unexpected places,*

*Volunteering their beauty for
those with eyes to see.*

*Like their creator, they smile
on the just and the unjust,*

*And bless the very ground
with their presence.*

*Strong, determined and free, they flourish
without help from a gardener's hand,*

*And know the exact moment to die.*

# Contact

**1st** World Library coordinates all of Brad Fregger's speaking engagements and offers seminars and workshops based on the concepts presented in Brad's two most recent books, *GET THINGS DONE – Ten Secrets of Creating and Leading Exceptional Teams*, and, *ONE SHOVEL FULL – Telling Stories to Change Beliefs, Attitudes, and Perceptions*.

**1st World Library** is an author services company designed to take advantage of the digital revolution in publishing and dedicated to providing the services authors need to get their books into publication.

"Through our combined experience, the skills of our people, the contributions of our partners, and the technology available today, we are able to provide authors who are interested in self-funding their book's publication, the best tools and experience available."

**1st World Library** assures its author-clients a quality product that meets the high standards of the publishing industry.

For additional information, see:
**http://www.1stworldlibrary.com**

**1st World Library**
8015 Shoal Creek Blvd., Suite 100
Austin, TX 78757
Voice: 512/339-4000
Fax: 512/458-1648
Email: **info@1stworldlibrary.com**

# Author's Bio

**B**rad Fregger, President/CEO of 1st World Library, has 45 years combined experience in retailing, corporate training, publishing, and software development. He is currently on the board of directors for two Internet companies and an adjunct professor at Saint Edward's University in Austin, Texas.

Brad is a practitioner/scholar, using the skills and knowledge he has learned to amass a remarkable record of accomplishment over the past 25 years. He's the founder of three major corporate training departments (Mervyn's, Atari, and Activision), and he's produced over 125 consumer and business products.

Brad's amazing ability to complete projects on time and on budget, plus his creative management style, caught the attention of Tom Peters (*In Search of Excellence*) who then featured Brad in his book, *Liberation Management*.

Brad is an expert in many critical areas of business, from customer service to management of technology. He presents talks and workshops, and has written three books: *LUCKY THAT WAY – Stories of Seizing the Moment While Creating the Games Millions Play*; *GET THINGS DONE – Ten Secrets of Creating and Leading Exceptional Teams*; and *ONE SHOVEL FULL – Telling Stories to Change Beliefs, Attitudes and Perceptions*.

Brad holds a Master's Degree in Futuristics. As an adjunct professor at the Graduate School of Management at Saint Edward's University, Brad both develops and teaches classes in the MBA (Introduction to eCommerce, Human Relations) and the Master of Science in Organizational Leadership & Ethics (Leadership & Imagination) programs.

Brad and his wife Barbara live outside Austin in the beautiful Texas hill country.

www.ingramcontent.com/pod-product-compliance
Lightning Source LLC
LaVergne TN
LVHW012009260326
834688LV00057B/356